SCATTERED
SHOTS

SCATTERED SHOTS

MAX HASTINGS

Line drawings by
William Geldart

MACMILLAN

First published 1999 by Macmillan
an imprint of Macmillan Publishers Ltd
25 Eccleston Place, London SW1W 9NF
Basingstoke and Oxford
Associated companies throughout the world
www.macmillan.co.uk

ISBN 0 333 77103 6

1 3 5 7 9 8 6 4 2

A CIP catalogue record for this book is available from
the British Library.

Phototypeset by Intype London Ltd
Printed and bound in Great Britain by
Mackays of Chatham plc, Chatham, Kent

To the memory of my father

MACDONALD HASTINGS

whose love for the English countryside inspired my own

CONTENTS

INTRODUCTION

EVERYBODY WHO HAS seen me shoot and fish knows how slight is the relationship between my enthusiasm for writing about country sports, and my ability to practise them. My role in life is to serve as standard-bearer and chief shop steward for sporting duffers. But the longer I go on contributing literary squibs about shooting and fishing, the more people who don't know me delude themselves that someone who expends so many words upon describing the pleasures of the countryside must know his stuff about them.

Not so, I fear, not so. You are reading the work of a man at times shaky about which tree is an ash and which an elm (presumably the dead one), who is still obliged to reach for *Collins Guide to British Birds* in order to tell one corvid from another. I fish – well, a bit better than I used to, because I get a fair amount of practice. But my casting in a wind can crack the stoniest Scots ghillie into mirth. My shooting is erratic. I have grown accustomed to the sardonic grins of new acquaintances who find themselves on the next peg to me, and who delight in observing how badly the game dealers are doing out of me, compared with the cartridge manufacturers.

The only sporting achievement I will boast freely about took place on a Saturday night last August, when I arrived back in London from Scotland, en route to a dawn flight for Italy. I had twenty-four grouse in my hand baggage. I suddenly realized that nowhere would I find anybody to dress them in London on a Saturday night, but I was damned if I was going to bin them. I sat down in my flat and plucked those birds out of sheer obstinacy. The job took four hours, and by the end there wasn't a room in the place without feathers in it. But every time a pink grouse touched my plate at home last winter I reminded myself that the ordeal had been worth it.

My claim upon the attention of readers, rural or otherwise, must rest upon my devotion to country pursuits, rather than my effectiveness with rod and gun. We won't even mention fox-hunting, nor tell the story of the day I caused a horse to fall down backwards. Hence the title of this collection. Aficionados of sporting literature will know that *Scattered Shots* is already to be found in some country libraries. It is a minor classic, indeed, written by one Major Jarvis, a governor of Sinai between the wars. Dear old Major Jarvis – who affected an ear trumpet, as would so many shooting people today if they were honest men – wrote with wit and affection about his sporting experiences at home and abroad. I feel he has now been sufficient years in his grave, and his book long enough out of print, to allow me to borrow his title. It offers an appropriate image of my own experiences.

Over the past twenty years, the fortunes of field sports in Britain have fluctuated. Shooting has expanded greatly, with more and more people eager to use a gun, and almost every acre of many counties 'in hand' for sporting purposes. There are more and more shooting enthusiasts every year. The disadvantage, however, is that the image of sport suffers from the adoption of driven-game shooting in places which are quite unsuitable for showing sporting birds, and from excess by some rich men.

I have to be honest here, and plead guilty to a measure of hypocrisy, because I take part in some big shoots. How many is 'too many'? Everybody's personal answer tends to be: a few more than one shoots oneself. But the image of shooting which the public thus embraces, of overweight aspiring toffs deposited by Range Rover at pegs where they stand with a flunkey or two and demolish hundreds of living creatures without risk or exertion, is ugly. It could undo game shooting in Britain in our lifetimes. Speaking personally, cross my heart, I would enjoy a lot of the days to which I am invited just as much if we shot half the number of birds. I do not think it is hair-splitting to add that, while it seems perfectly reasonable to use flags and flankers to turn birds, at some shoots it is depressing to see flaggers standing between cover and guns, to persuade the wretched birds to rise to a height at which they may safely, never mind sportingly, be shot.

In recent years, fishermen have seen hostility to their sport grow among 'animal rights' enthusiasts. But far more alarming has been the decline in wild sport: falling salmon catches all over the British Isles. The chief culprit, evidence overwhelmingly suggests, is netting at sea. It seems remarkable that successive British governments dally with restrictions upon rod and line fishing, while declining to act against industrial and drift-net fishing, which inflict far greater environmental damage. Here at home, the tragedy is compounded by man-made follies: forestry and fish-farming. The evidence is plain, that hill drainage and acidification caused by subsidized softwood planting have inflicted awful damage on Scottish fishing. Likewise, the pollution generated by inshore salmon farms has had a fearful impact. No minister seems willing to confront these issues, because jobs and votes are thought to be at stake in Scotland, where local politics are anyway explosive. Inshore fish-farms are now proven to create breeding grounds for disease. They strip the seabed of natural life. The disaster is compounded

on the margin by the unchecked proliferation of seals, and
the protection granted to cormorants and other winged
predators. The hapless salmon has become a victim of the
public's arbitrary support for certain species as against
others. Fish command none of the popular enthusiasm generated by furry and winged creatures. The beauty of a spring
salmon possesses no magic for members of the RSPB – or
for most politicians. The problem for Scottish salmon is
that their interests are thought to be merely those of rich
anglers who can afford to fish for them, with whom the
mood of the times is out of sympathy. There is a visceral
belief that a sport which people pay thousands of pounds
to enjoy can scarcely march with the public interest –
certainly not with the Scottish public interest, when so
many salmon anglers are English. Michael Wigan, himself
a landowner on a Scottish river-bank, has written bitterly
about 'the popular demonology of the landowner as a selfish
pleasure seeker . . . It has become almost inconceivable for
any figure in the public domain to come out in support of
sporting use.'

Scotland has been the happy hunting ground of so many
of us for so long that it is tragic to behold the battles which
now beset the Highlands. No Englishman loves Scotland
more than I do, nor is more grieved by what is happening
up there. But it seems essential to admit the existence of a
problem in order to have any hope of addressing it. In the
summer of 1996, I suggested that the English should face
the fact that we and our sporting enthusiasms have become
seriously unpopular in Scotland. When my article appeared
in the *Field* there was uproar. Some old friends expressed
either passionate disbelief in my argument or anger that I
had raised a spectre which should have been kept under
wraps. The Scottish newspapers, which widely reported

what I wrote, wilfully misrepresented it as an attack on 'whinging Scots'.

In truth, I was seeking simply to focus attention on a reality that seemed inescapable: however doubtful the economic and political reasoning behind it, impatience with English rule and English land ownership in Scotland has been growing steadily and is approaching boiling point. Friends who said crossly to me, '*Our* keepers/*our* ghillies have always adored us,' were missing the point about the mood in many Highland communities, granted that sentiment varies widely from area to area. The wipe-out of the Conservatives in Scotland at the 1997 election, which I won a few bets by anticipating, seemed merely to confirm a trend which has profound implications for sport in this island. Resentment of private management of our great wildernesses, allied to ignorance of nature and agricultural economics, a touch of the politics of envy and nationalism, together with campaigning by environmental groups who should know better, cast a long shadow over field sports in the Highlands. Many of us enjoy Scotland as much as ever. But political radicalism poses a threat to the great heritage of Scottish field sports, whose full impact has yet to be felt.

The fox-hunters are basking in a reprieve from the immediate threat of legislation, following the failure of the Foster bill in the spring of 1998. Yet we must never blind ourselves to the strength of hostile opinion on this issue. Those of us who merely get on with enjoying our own lives, and feel no interest in crusading to interfere with other people's, are bemused by the obsession of those who oppose fox-hunting. What kind of country are we, in which MPs can work themselves into a fever and devote so much time and energy to preserving an animal pest, when there is so much to be done to improve the lot of mankind? If parliament generated half as much passion in debating the

welfare of, say, children in care, some MPs' priorities might
seem saner. We were all heartened by the turnout and the
dignity of the Countryside March in March 1998. It was
important. It made a difference. It impressed, even alarmed,
Labour ministers. But we shall need to do it again, with
more people. We can never afford to forget how great is
the weight of public sentiment in Britain today against
field sports in general, and fox-hunting in particular. Some
hunts continue to behave with remarkable insensitivity,
given the climate of public opinion. Sensible fox-hunters
recognize that they are walking on eggshells, especially now
that almost all the hereditary peers in the House of
Commons are losing their voting rights.

We have become, in a host of ways, a people moved by
sentiment rather than rationality. Our emotional lurches are
fed by politicians and the media. We shall be a poorer and
greyer society if fox-hunting is abolished. It is encouraging
that some senior Labour ministers, such as Jack Straw,
oppose legislation not because they care for hunting, but
because they recognize the threat to personal liberty which
a ban would represent. What would it say about the sort
of society we are, if parliament sets about abolishing every
minority activity with which some people are out of sympathy? Yet we face a hard struggle to preserve fox-hunting.
Fox-hunters sometimes accuse their opponents of being
prompted by ignorance of the issues. They suggest that if
the critics knew more about the reality of hunting, they
would change their view. This is true of some 'antis'. But
it is almost impossible for the supporters of field sports to
conduct an argument with those – a growing number –
who simply think that it is wrong for humans to gain
pleasure from the pursuit of wild creatures. The chasm
between their view of the hierarchy of natural behaviour
and ours is too wide to bridge. It is the misfortune of fox-

hunting to be, by its nature, the most conspicuous country sport. The images that conjure up a great historic, rural pageant for its admirers seem to its opponents the essence of cruelty.

But *courage, mes braves*! Amid all the fears about troubles ahead, it is remarkable how many peerless pleasures remain in Britain's countryside, in defiance of the expectations of our parents and grandparents, who thought they would vanish long ago. Even amid the decline of Scottish salmon, I was lucky enough to land seven in two days on Tweed last October. The chalk streams of southern England, which have languished in recent years due to the reckless abstraction policies of Thames Water and its brethren, were so revived by rain that they yielded wonderful fishing throughout the summers of 1998 and 1999. For all the problems stalking and shooting face, every season many of us enjoy marvellous days on the hill and in the woods. The fight for the cause of field sports will continue from year to year and ditch to ditch, but today we can rejoice in the richness all around us, of which this book is intended as a modest reflection.

James Wilson wrote a work called *Rod and Gun* in 1840, in which he declared that 'in sound or simple truth, writing of a book on almost any subject is humbug'. Being a verbose Victorian, he went on to suggest that 'pleasure, pride, poverty, happiness, hunger, anger, disdain, contempt, candour, fear, love, hatred, hope, knowledge, malice, misery, dissimulation, philanthropy, philoprogenitiveness, conceit, arrogance, ignorance – these are a few of the many fertile sources from which the things called books are ever flowing'. I hope my own motives are not quite as complex as those Mr Wilson proposes, but all authors must plead guilty to some of them, and apologize accordingly.

I owe thanks to the editor of the *Field*, the splendid

Jonathan Young, who first published many of the words which follow. Those who endure my company on the riverbank or in the shooting field are a forbearing and kindly lot, to whom I am always indebted. My children, whose enthusiasm for field sports waxes and wanes from season to season, think they deserve my gratitude for putting up with their father talking and writing so much about these things. My wife Penny, who has accompanied me on so many sporting expeditions with good cheer, patience, sympathy and wit, has earned the most heartfelt bouquet of all. Whenever I look out of a London office window, and suffer even a twinge of self-pity for my semi-urban lot, I can cheer myself at once by conjuring a vision of the next cast on the Helmsdale, the next covey exploding over a grouse butt, the next sortie on a frosty December stubble in happy company. This book is for all those who share my delight in the countryside of these islands.

MAX HASTINGS
HAYWARD HOUSE, BERKSHIRE
JULY 1999

1

FARMED OUT

IT IS A symptom of middle age to discover that common-
places of one's childhood have achieved museum status. At
a country show a few months ago, I pottered through a
display of vintage agricultural machinery. I do not think of
myself as very old, yet I can remember seeing most of those
antiques going about their business in the fields of Berkshire
in the early 1950s. The throaty chuckle of the post-war
Fordson tractor, with the oval fuel tank atop the engine,
was unforgettable. The stately whirl of the binder arms
possessed a grace curiously at odds with the clatter of the
threshing machine to which its sheaves were consigned.

In the days when farm labour was still plentiful – and needed to be – I worked for a few weeks on a towed combine harvester, which required a man on a platform at the back bagging the threshed corn as the machine rolled across the field. I loved to stand on the sledge towed behind the baler, alongside the man who stacked bales as the straw surged out of the chute. Farmhands were not gentle – why should they have been? – with young middle-class interlopers like me, who scrambled on to the ricks as they were taken down by a sweating gang of shirtless men. I sobbed my heart out after one of them stuffed the wriggling contents of a rat's nest into my nine-year-old shirt.

Later, in my teens, some farmers were rash enough to let me work for them in the school holidays. Today, everybody is obsessively cautious about allowing children near high-tech machinery. Boys routinely ploughed and harrowed thirty-five years ago. Nobody saw anything unreasonable about letting the likes of me loose at the wheel of a tractor, to steer an erratic furrow. Dexterity was never my best thing. Bale stacks which I assembled had a habit of collapsing. One day I was helping a farmer fit a new razor blade in the grass cutter. It jammed inexplicably. Only after several seconds did we grasp that the obstacle was the index finger of my right hand, where the blade was firmly wedged against the bone. I bear the scar to this day. Nor was it only my flesh and bone which suffered. At a tender age, I demonstrated a facility for smashing the most robust machinery: a muck spreader paid a stiff price for clumsy handling one summer morning. The only occasion that I can remember seeing a farmer remove his cap and scratch his head in approved caricature rustic manner occurred when he discovered that I had shattered a massive agricultural roller in a few minutes of careless driving. Fortunately, there were enough farmers in our part of the world, who did not communicate regularly with each other, to enable me to find successive employers through several summers.

Do farmyards still seem magical playgrounds to a new generation of children, tobogganing among the bale stacks and burrowing among the rafters at the summits of the great straw mountains? I don't think so. Unless one is a farmer's child, everybody has had to become much more 'responsible' about the custody of farm equipment. Few people these days dare to let children ride as passengers on combine harvesters or drive those huge tractors with computerized instrument panels, a far cry from the old Fordson Major whose hydraulic hitch seemed to represent space-age technology forty years ago.

I suppose we should all welcome the transformation of hygiene standards, to which our parents' generation adopted such a cavalier attitude. I remember hand milking one summer on a small farm in the Highlands, where nobody gave a thought to washing their hands, any more than the shepherd cleaned his clasp-knife before he butchered a lamb in the outside shed, while we watched with morbid fascination. Impressed though we all are by New Age hygiene, our obsession with sterilization must be killing off natural resistance to microbes a good deal quicker than you can say BSE. I am a fan of Patrick O'Brian's great novels about Nelson's navy. I often ask myself how those doughty old salts managed to live to a ripe age on beef three years in the cask and biscuits teeming with weevils, without a single member of the Health and Safety police in sight.

Every year, we become a more relentlessly organized and regulated society. In consequence, each of us exists in a specialized capsule, with less and less knowledge of other people's lives. Although some of my own upbringing was urban, I was able to learn a lot about farming life – far more than has come the way of my own country-bred children. The law becomes an ever more formidable impediment to dabbling in other people's business. Thirty years ago on a visit to the vast King Ranch in Texas I asked if I could try one of their famous quarter horses. The wrangler asked, 'Are you insured?'

I looked blank.

'Well, we can hardly let you ride our horses unless you're insured.'

'But I'm not going to sue you if I fall off.'

'Everybody else does.'

That conversation mystified me, fresh from England. Today, God help us, the same could happen in this country. Liability has become an obsession, fuelled by greedy lawyers and foolish judges and juries prepared to encourage plaintiffs to pursue their 'rights' beyond the limits of sanity. The consequence is that no employer can afford to take risks any more. Some farmers growing specialized crops still employ seasonal fruit pickers and suchlike, but most agricultural equipment demands highly skilled operators. The notion of letting a schoolboy loose on a piece of kit that costs hundreds of thousands of pounds, quite apart from the legal risk, is out of sight.

But the next generation will miss the fun we had playing in the farmyard. I discovered a sense of romance and excitement about the scent of hay, the clatter of the baler, playing catch-as-catch-can with sheep at the dipper, driving Anguses from field to field. I would never pretend that I became a genuinely rural child, nor even that I got along very well with the farmworkers and their offspring. But I learnt enough to feel at home with the sights and sounds and smells of rural life. Many of my generation of middle-class children did likewise. Today, by contrast, when agriculture has become a controversial and even unpopular business, the industry loses a lot because a diminishing number of outsiders know anything about it. Intensive farming has had some disastrous consequences for the environment, but these were the result of a centrally directed, government-inspired policy to produce food at all costs, of which farmers were only the instruments. No individual could resist the nationwide trend if he wanted to stay in business.

Farmers, who have spent much of their lives being treated as useful members of the community, are bemused to find themselves widely regarded not only as despoilers of the land through intensive husbandry, but also as leeches upon the taxpayer who funds them. For forty years, during and after the Second World War, the public was taught to applaud farmers as the producers of our food. Agriculture was the most highly directed industry in Britain. Little or nothing was said about subsidy. Farmers were getting public money, but successive governments considered this an acceptable price for boosting food production. Now, however, the urban population is acutely aware of the vast sums of their money which are poured into farming, and they are resentful.

It is true that subsidy has for years enabled big farmers to grow richer than the real economic contribution they make could justify, and has kept alive a belief among small farmers that they should expect a living from acreages which are simply not viable. This is not their fault, and the current campaign against farmers ignores the fact that many have sincerely striven to be responsible stewards of their lands for generations. But the combination of production surpluses, environmental damage and continuing subsidy contribute greatly to the difficulties of making the case for the country-side, and for country sports. Yes, we know that over the past three years agricultural incomes have fallen dramatically. But for decades before that the money was pouring in, and the public has little sympathy.

Subsidy provides a political justification for urban and suburban politicians to ride roughshod over the countryside and its ways, in a fashion that would have been unthinkable a generation ago. What has changed is not so much the townsman's view of country life, as his perceived right to interfere with it. Even a century ago, many people who did not hunt or shoot felt as much revulsion towards the hunters' and shooters' enthusiasm for killing animals for pleasure as do their modern counterparts. Mr Pooter and his friends in Brickfield Terrace shuddered as deeply at the notion of a hunted fox as does, say, Ann Widdecombe today.

But for hundreds of years, even in the most aggressively urban circles, the rights of a landowner to do as he chose on his own acres were not much disputed. Farmers might be perceived in the city as alien creatures whose ways were not urban ways, but they were respected as the people who grew the nation's food.

Today, the public may not know that one of the wealthiest peers in the land boasted at the bar of White's that his annual set-aside cheque has been running at over £1 million, but they get the general idea. They know all about the EU's mountains. They know that much of the corn they see in the fields is not needed by our society. They are repelled by the chemical and industrial demands of intensive cultivation, and they do not readily understand why it is so hard to abandon these practices as long as others are employing them. They question the integrity of landowners as stewards, when many have seized every opportunity to enrich themselves by selling off land for development. In consequence, many people believe they have a legitimate stake in the landowner's broad acres, and the way he tends them, through the subsidies they give him as taxpayers.

Egged on by aggressive lobbies such as the Ramblers' Association and the RSPB, they are no longer willing to respect the traditional self-governance of farmers and country dwellers. The new awareness of public subsidy of agriculture has fired an Exocet through the historic concept of private ownership. An articulate part of the urban public is determined to assert its own view about how rural life should be conducted. Take badgers. The veterinary advice is overwhelming: badgers spread bovine tuberculosis and if populations of infected badgers are left unchecked, farmers in affected areas can lose their livelihoods. Yet the 'animal welfare' lobby remains resolute in its resistance to culling infected badgers, with the implicit message that the farmers and their beasts can go hang.

It has been plain for years that country interests must make concessions on the issue of public access. Enlightened landowners have already done so. Yet farmers justly resist the idea of an absolute 'right to roam', of a notion that anyone should be allowed to go anywhere at any time in the countryside; they have evidence to support them about what a menace unchecked urban visitors can be. There is a vague public belief that agricultural production has become a redundant activity, that the whole countryside over the next generation or two can become a giant park. In reality, of course, surpluses or no surpluses, subsidy or no subsidy, most of rural Britain must continue to be profitably farmed. It will remain a factory floor, where unchecked public access is not only unwise but actively dangerous.

Unfortunately, the Government is more sympathetic to the likes of the Ramblers. Ministers are surely right to argue that there must be a change in the pattern of agricultural subsidy, to favour the environment and provide social support for keeping small farmers on the land, rather than to encourage mere production. But they seem insensitive when they talk as if this can be accomplished at a stroke. Agriculture is above all about continuity and the long term. It runs deeply against the interests of the British countryside, as well as those of farmers, to suggest that policy can be wrenched in one direction or another without years of warning and planning.

Yet some country dwellers delude themselves by supposing that only a few left-wing politicians and media people are against them, while most of the public remains on their side. In reality, many town dwellers of all political persuasions are today antipathetic to traditional country ways. Few urban or suburban dwellers will lift a finger, or rather a vote, on behalf of the countryside and country sports. The countryside enjoys public support only in terms defined by professional environmentalists. Sentimentality, such a powerful and dangerous driving force in so many aspects of British life, poses one of the greatest threats to the countryside. The historian John Keegan remarked recently that he, like most of his generation, had been brought up to suppose that the whole purpose of education was to inspire respect for rationality rather than sentiment. Yet now, he observed, many people want to argue as if instinct was not merely of comparable value to reason, but its moral superior. Nowhere has this change of values made more impact than in the debate on the countryside. Sentiment, rather than the fruit of logic or research, increasingly holds sway in dictating urban and political attitudes.

More, this approach extends to some powerful lobbies which purport to serve the cause of nature. The day the RSPB abandoned the culling of vermin on its reserve at Abernethy because its members do not like the practice, the organization signalled to the world that the values – the very richly funded values – of suburban Britain dominate its attitude to conservation. A countryman who knocks an injured bird on the head is thought uncharitable, even brutal, alongside the passer-by who picks it up and takes it to an 'animal hospital'. The same passer-by probably chooses to be oblivious to the fact that the domestic cat now poses the biggest single threat to our wild songbird population. One of the defining characteristics of the traditional countryside is that people treat animals with respect and compassion, but without sentimentality. To 'animal rights' supporters, this is not good enough. The countryside must be taught or compelled to behave better. A growing number of politicians advance the banner for this view. With feelings heightened by such controversies as those about raptor control, animal feeds and agricultural pollution, the word has gone out from Westminster and Whitehall that rural people can no longer be trusted to manage their own affairs.

The countryside no longer possesses anything like the clout which it could claim as late as the 1970s. In France, enough of a genuine peasant culture survives to give French farmers substantial political power. In Britain, there is no peasant culture. Big landowners dominate public and political perception, to the fury of small farmers. Now that political as well as social power is slipping away from the landowning aristocracy, their traditional enthusiasms and interests have become Aunt Sallys for all manner of hostile lobbies. Perception is all, especially amid a hostile media. It seems essential for the future of the countryside, as well as of field sports, that their interests should be seen to be represented by non-toffs, by 'ordinary people', to use an invidious but popular phrase.

Matthew Parris wrote an article in *The Times* a year or two ago in which he suggested that private gun ownership in Britain would sooner or later be ended. Such a development would not reflect his own wishes, he said. He does not care about the matter one way or the other. This is merely his view of the way the public mood is going. Parris is a shrewd commentator. The shift in attitudes about which he wrote is not politically partisan. It has little to do with which government is in power, for heaven knows the Tories have shown little sympathy for rural issues in recent years. It simply reflects the shift of public sentiment.

Sentiment can change. In 1945 our grandparents believed the game was up for traditional country life and pastimes. Happily they were proved wrong. The same could happen again. But for this to become possible it seems important to deny the urban majority, and the House of Commons which overwhelmingly reflects its will, the economic basis for its claim to tell the countryside how to go about its business. Voters must not be able to argue that landowners and farmers are leeches upon the public purse. Plainly, British farmers cannot operate at world market prices if their European competitors are not doing likewise, but reform of the CAP has to come. Subsidy will shift from production to social and environmental purposes. This is surely in the best interests of the countryside. If agriculture was seen by the urban and suburban public to be paying its own way, country people could fight far more effectively for the right to lead country life on their own terms. As long as the urban public is bankrolling the rural population through subsidy, as long as Brussels and thus the British taxpayer are perceived to be paying for so many people's cartridges, the urban public will claim the right to call the tune.

2

THE SHEEN OF THE SPRINGER

SCOTTISH SUMMER FISHING has yielded so many disappointments in recent years, with shrunken rivers desperate for rain and taking fish, that I have changed gear to become a spring fisher again. The price, we know, is that one misses the bonanzas which sometimes come in June or July. There are fewer fish to be caught in May, and recent Mays in Scotland have been disappointing. But what fish! After an absence of five or six years from spring Scottish rivers, it is a joy once more to see those gleaming silver and blue salmon, to feel their power at the other end of a bent rod and taut line.

I set out for the Helmsdale on a spring morning with
an armoury of heavy tubes which never left the box. The
water was at a good summer height and demanded nothing
bigger than a two-inch treble. On the first day I got into
a fish within a couple of casts, and had him on for a minute
before the rod straightened. Then he was gone, for no
special reason that either I or young George the ghillie
could divine. Neither of us was downhearted. I was excited
to have met a fish so soon. On a sharp, clear day with the
sun shining, there seemed nothing to moan about. After so
many summer experiences of fishing in low water, I revelled
in the pleasure of watching a strong, steady, glittering
stream flow down the strath, the fly drifting plausibly across
it at every cast.

It was not so easy in the falls pools, where the fly circled
back with the eddies in all manner of manoeuvres unlikely
to tempt a fish. But young George was in confident mood.
At every pool he would say, 'It looks perfect. We've got to
have a fish out of here today.' In the event, it was late
afternoon and I was growing weary and maybe even a touch
despondent when, in the midst of a long, flat stretch of
wading, a fish took. I knew at once that it was a good one.
The salmon tore away downstream, and I sploshed clumsily
out of the water to follow it, thrilling to that matchless
sensation as I stumbled along the bank.

It took twenty minutes to land it, at least five longer
than George thought necessary. But the first fish of the
week, the first of the year, is the one you never want to
lose. It was 14lb and in perfect condition. I sat on the bank
marvelling at its colours for several minutes after we lifted
it out. To paraphrase Ratty, there is nothing, absolutely
nothing to beat the beauty of a spring salmon – and I got
another the next morning.

In the days that followed on the Helmsdale and the

Naver, I was reminded what a tough business spring fishing can be. The weather was cold, the wind fierce, sometimes to gale force. It was all but impossible to cast a line in a manner any fish would respect. Two days running, even in the heaviest waterproofs, we squelched home soaked to the bone. We did not need chest waders for wading, but how helpful they can be to keep out the rain! The birds were perfect, the sandpipers and geese and curlews and, above all, oystercatchers. Fishing a Naver pool one morning, I was dive-bombed again and again by an anxious nesting oystercatcher, which often closed to within three or four feet. I grew far more interested in her antics than in those of the invisible salmon. It grows depressing, casting hour after hour without seeing a fish show – but then again, we know how frustrating it can also be in high summer to see everywhere salmon showing which scorn a fly.

One evening on the Naver, to my exasperation I lost two fish inside five minutes in the same pool. The first was the less emotional experience, because it only had time to pull out three or four yards of line before it was gone. The second encounter was more dramatic. A 10lb salmon seized a small Willie Gunn and tore upstream until, immediately opposite me, it sprang from the water and hung for a second in the air before my eyes, shaking its head and my fly, before plunging once more into the current to freedom.

I was so moved by the sight that I muffled my own disappointment until I met my companion, proudly clutching an eleven-pounder, the first fish he had landed alone. When the congratulations were over, I felt cross with myself for having bungled things, a sensation not diminished next day when I again returned empty-handed, while my fellow fisher landed another. One wonders what one is doing wrong. The only way to recover confidence is to catch another fish.

My last morning in Sutherland broke into perfect spring sunshine with eight inches of water on the gauge. We were on six, the best beat on the river. A quarter of an hour into my first pool, that lovely stretch the Crooked Stream, a fish took me, which spent the next ten minutes performing every acrobatic in the hooked salmon's repertory. Watching that shimmering body twist brilliantly just below the sunlit brown surface of the river, I wanted the experience never to end. At last I netted 13lb of silver fish. Its sea lice still possessed their tails. Donald the ghillie said, 'That fish will have come in on last night's tide.' The romance seemed irresistible, of catching in the bright water a fish only hours in from the sea. I set off home perfectly content.

I can't deny that some of those May days seemed depressing, as we cast across apparently empty pools in lashing rain and wind. But the prizes are marvellous and the pleasure is so great of seeing rivers at their best, with current spilling over the banks. I shall be back, even if the big hitters among anglers, the men and women who land the jumbo catches in high summer, sneer at how little it takes to keep a spring fisher happy.

3

FATHERS AND SONS

WHEN I WAS a child, although I was very keen on field sports, I had few opportunities to practise them. At the age of nine, one February evening my father took me pigeon shooting for the first time, in some beech woods near our Berkshire cottage. 'You put yourself there,' said Father, appointing me to a large bramble patch. I was left in shivering solitude to contemplate life as it came on to snow, feeling like Mole on a bad day in the Wild Wood. I was armed, bored, cold and impatient to let off the gun. A bird suddenly stirred in front of me in the twilight, with a great bustle and flutter of wings. I fired into the gloom at a point perhaps three feet above the ground, and shouted proudly, 'Daddy! I've shot something!' My father explored the brambles and reappeared clutching a dead hen pheasant. 'This had better go in here,' he muttered, transferring the corpse to a poacher's pocket. There was a distinct lack of congratulation, and a casserole a week later. But any day thereafter, I leapt at the chance to go out shooting. The sport was imbued with a thrill, a specialness in my life which it has never lost. As a teenager, I happily bicycled miles for the chance to walk a few hedgerows with a gun, or to cast a clumsy fly over the dace in a Surrey stream. I yearned in vain for Scottish lodges, salmon rivers and grouse moors. Consequently, years later when I gained keys to these things, I valued them beyond price – as I still do.

My own children are different. They have had all sorts of opportunities to shoot and fish, and as a result take them somewhat for granted. 'What do you expect us to say, Daddy?' demanded my elder son, when I once harangued him about how grateful he should be for a glorious Highland holiday. 'We've never known anything else.' The younger Hastingses have had little experience of rough-shooting. I made the mistake of introducing them to driven game much too soon. Most of us try to give our children what we did not have ourselves. I regret that they have not often shared the fun of walking hedges and ditches for small return.

My 22-year-old daughter decided a while ago that she does not care for Scottish holidays. She shoots occasionally if she happens to be around when we have a day, but is then surprised to discover that, without regular practice, she does not hit a lot. My elder son, twenty-six, picks up the occasional rod or gun, but is happier on pavements. Only my younger son, now sixteen, cherishes an enthusiastic blood-lust. On the river, even when it is my fly that has hooked the fish, I hear the cry go up as I lift the net: 'Please can I kill it?' Friends enquire innocently from whom he could have inherited this attitude.

There are plenty of keen young fishers and shots about the place. But I am not sure that the next generation, even the country-reared part of it, will adopt as uncomplicated and unsentimental an attitude towards field sports as our own has done. The young are intensively propagandized from an early age about the iniquities of cruelty to wildlife. They are growing up in an age in which conservation is an increasing preoccupation of Western society. Most of us energetically preach the message that field sports are vital to conservation, and there is plenty of evidence to support the argument, but some of our children are more prone than we were to flinch from perceived cruelties. Their urban contemporaries shudder at the mention of shooting or even fishing. Over the years, children's exposure to relentless media and public criticism of country sports must have some cumulative effect. Some teenagers become liable to question whether the manner in which daddy spends his leisure hours is civilized, decent or humane. I admire the work done by the Countryside Foundation to get sensible information about country life and field sports into schools, but it is a struggle. Most schoolteachers are instinctively unsympathetic.

At home it seems most sensible to argue the conservation case patiently, and to give children the opportunity to participate in field sports without pressuring them to do so. My daughter stopped hunting for several years but went out for the odd day last season and was surprised how much she enjoyed herself. I suspect she will discover the bliss of Scotland if she finds herself with a keen sporting boyfriend. It is more persuasive to point out the social perks of field sports, than to wax sanctimonious about the need to control deer. I offer the same message to all my lot: if you want to do these things, they are there. But if not, go clubbing or lie on the beach — it's your life.

Proficiency, or lack of it, plays some part in how most children feel. I remember how equivocal I became about shooting for some time when I was young because I was such a very bad shot. I see my children going through the same exasperation when they miss things, or cannot cast a long enough line to catch a fish. Some children shoot or fish superbly, but these are a minority, and tend to be drawn from families who own coverts or rivers. Most do not become competent until they are in their late teens, at least. My elder son throws a better salmon line than I do, but so far he has been less lucky in what he catches. A few years ago we shared a wonderful spate on the Helmsdale. Although we both caught a lot of fish, he ended one day demanding in exasperation, 'Why do you catch bigger fish than I do?' I pointed out gently that no fisherman yet born can dictate the size of the catch. I added that I was fifteen years older than he was when I landed my first salmon. He was not impressed. Nothing turns off any boy quicker than a sentence which starts, 'When I was your age . . .'

Each generation has to reconcile itself to the indifference of its successors to what has gone before. Children rarely perceive parental experience as relevant to their own, at least until it is too late. Our generation grew up in a world in which military prowess was esteemed, and many of us yearned to go forth in search of adventures, in the approved manner of G. A. Henty. Today, few people under thirty have even met any soldiers or former soldiers. Their idols were not formed on battlefields, nor even perhaps on phea-sant drives. They do not perceive themselves as specially lucky or privileged, but then I suppose one never does. My father was always telling me how lucky I was, and of course

I never believed a word of it either. He talked endlessly of a future gaffing my salmon, though he was never to do so. I, on the other hand, found myself netting fish and retrieving birds for my own children from their earliest years. Such moments give any sporting father exquisite pleasure. As a parent, however, one cannot claim much credit for taking children out to do things one enjoys oneself. My offspring may be right to feel that they don't have to be too grateful to me for taking them shooting and fishing, because I am, after all, pleasing myself. Now that they are mostly grown-up, I never pressure them about their own sports and pastimes. But like every sporting father, I shall be a sad man a decade or two hence, if at least one of my own brood does not carry on a family tradition.

4

HERE BE MONSTERS

ONE DAY RECENTLY a north-eastern motor tycoon arranged a shoot for himself near his home. 'For himself' were the operative words. He turned up alone at 9.15 a.m., solemnly stood through five drives during which he killed 250-odd pheasants, and then went home, to all appearances perfectly satisfied. Indeed he must have enjoyed the outing because a week or two later he arranged another. The estate's owner, happy to bank his cheques, enquired, deadpan, whether he would be wanting his usual lunch table for one; his guest acceded.

On the day, however, matters turned nasty. 'I shall stand

here,' said the vastly rich, lone tenant before the first drive. 'No sir, you will stand *there*,' said the keeper firmly, as befitted a Northumbrian who thoroughly understood his own business. To cut a long story short, the debate about where the solitary peg should stand proved irreconcilable. After some increasingly acrimonious exchanges, the tenant went home in high dudgeon, leaving the pickers-up, keepers and so on to amuse themselves however they saw fit.

Now, you may think this story is a figment of my over-fertile imagination. It is not. There have been fevered discussions in shooting circles ever since about the behaviour of the tycoon concerned. How could a solitary day of that kind give pleasure? A friend said, 'It's like giving a cocktail party and only asking yourself.' But the man responsible was a lifelong rival of Sir Joseph Nickerson, a man of equally manic sporting habits, who also enjoyed this sort of extravagance. I suspect that the Northumbrian tenant was demonstrating to himself that anything Nickerson could do, he could do better. However, another friend of mine has a simpler explanation: 'This chap simply regards taking a solo, 250-bird day the way you or I might treat a trip to the shooting school.'

Anyway, this business set me thinking about the things that make or break a shooting day. The formidable, elderly widow of a Berkshire landowner came up to me at a cocktail party recently and introduced herself with the intriguing one-liner: 'Your father shot my husband.' For a moment, I was uncertain whether she was about to demand that I give her son immediate satisfaction on the lawn outside, or to express her gratitude towards my father for removing the chief obstacle to her happiness.

In the event, fortunately, neither proved appropriate. She explained how trivial and entertaining the whole episode had been. Well, er, yes. All shooters live in dread of shooting somebody, chiefly because, unless one is incredibly grand, nobody laughs. I have been shot several times. Friends say that, given the provocation I provide, it is astonishing that no incident has yet proved fatal. On the last occasion, in a grouse butt, I took a couple of pellets in the leg which stung no end. Having established that gangrene was unlikely, I did not say a lot, because loud protests tend to cast a damper over the day. It was my host's son who did it, and I wanted to be asked again. The culprit no doubt consoled himself with James I's remark, on hearing news that his Archbishop of Canterbury, a notoriously dangerous shot, had felled a keeper named Peter Hawkins in mistake for a buck, at Bramshill in Hampshire on 24 July 1621. 'An angel might have miscarried in that sort,' smiled the King indulgently. But if one is not a king, one is liable to feel a bit cross, and even frightened, when these things happen.

On a lighter note, there is no end of argument on shooting days about alleged poaching of other people's birds. It is amazing how often tempers are lost. In Wiltshire one day last season, I found myself standing next to an American lawyer who lives in England and has sought to make himself a big noise in the sporting world. The first couple of partridges he shot off my head I thought might only be accidents. I remonstrated mildly after the next two. Then I realized that he intended to do this *all the time*. He made the rest of the day a nightmare. I can get a gun up quite quick, but beating him to the draw was tough. To make matters worse, he shot very straight. Most of what he fired at in front of me, he killed. Retaliation was tough. The only thing I had a good chance of destroying on his peg was himself, and American lawyers have such litigious next-of-kin, don't y'know. At the end of the day, apparently oblivious of my rage, he suggested that we might get together some time. Between clenched teeth, I muttered something about dawn, and swords and pistols. But if we end up at twenty paces, this brute would get his shot off before I had my pistol out of the case.

Monarchs and princes, whether of nations or industries, get into the habit of expecting matters to go their own way and become pretty crotchety if they don't. I like a story I heard the other day about the current King of Spain, shooting in England and as usual being placed in the middle of the line for every drive. A neighbour was a trifle miffed to find that, even on the plum peg, the King mowed down a succession of birds heading for next door. When the whistle went, the King marched towards him. My friend absurdly fancied he was about to get an apology. Ho, ho. The King was cross. 'Did you *see* that man on my other side? He kept poaching my birds.' You can't win with kings.

Seriously, though, at some shoots the pegs are so close together that it is impossible to judge accurately who should take a given pheasant. We have all read stories about how a covey of eight grouse flew between Lords Walsingham and De Grey, and they killed the lot because each gun perfectly understood which birds belonged to him. I have never believed a word of it, not least because the two men concerned were legends for sporting greed, as well as prowess. How can one always know?

At very high bird shoots in Devon and Yorkshire, local rules tend to support the view that whichever gun thinks he can take a shot at a pheasant should do so. If you hesitate, by the time you've worked out the niceties about which of you is directly underneath some oxygen-breathing superbird half a mile up, it is already over the next valley. At a lot of drives on a lot of shoots, a neighbouring gun can often get a more sporting shot at a bird than the man underneath

it. Only the most tiresome martinet can mind. One day
in Durham, however, a notoriously bloody-minded guest
insisted on having his neighbour's cartridge cases counted
to support his claim that the neighbour had been poaching.
To his embarrassment, the victim of his wrath was proved
to have fired rather fewer cartridges than he had done
himself.

The best way of avoiding poaching arguments is to be
sure of the ground rules between neighbours before a drive
begins. I have poached accidentally many times, but only
once deliberately. I was standing next to a choleric old peer
who proceeded to mow down any birds heading my way
all morning. Later on, we stood in a valley where every bird
coming towards him had to make a diagonal across me.
Suddenly, mischief lent unusual brilliance to my performance. I destroyed almost everything in his path. He
complained bitterly at lunch to my host, a good-natured
fellow. I explained that I would like the old boy to know
that I had not done it by accident. We have glowered at
each other every time we have met since.

Lunch is a milestone in any shooting day, which contributes almost as much as the birds to whether we enjoy
ourselves. It can also be competitive. In my early twenties,
when parties of us used to bring our own packed lunches
to eat in a barn between swamps and walked-up sugar beet,
nobody minded much who had seen most pheasants. But
you could cut the atmosphere with a knife, between the
men who unrolled potted shrimps, hot sausages and stilton,
as against the hapless victims of wives who supplied only
a lump of nondescript cheddar and an apple.

The Edwardians overdid lunch as much as they overdid
their bags. It was fashionable to erect a marquee in the
middle of nowhere, to create a semblance of a picnic atmosphere, while providing the sort of fare one might expect to

be offered on a feast day at the Ritz. At most shoots in our own times the venues vary. Some estates possess purpose-built lunch huts or even lunch houses. Where the host is on his own home ground, one may be invited into the house or the stables. This usually makes for a better lunch but also involves removing boots and Barbours, brushing hair and donning tweed jackets. I am one of the natural philistines who feels that taking off a cartridge belt represents grooming enough. My dog agrees, and prefers alfresco lunches where he can profit from everybody's discards.

It is unusual for any lunch to start with a full complement of guns. At least one guest, in the sort of company I keep, is out looking for a pheasant or a dog when the stew is served. I have known there to be an odd body still standing hopefully on his peg in the spinneys, waiting to hear the whistle for the end of the drive, when a mile away the port is going round. The reverse can also be true. A year or two ago, I was shivering on the point of a wood quite close to the house, at the end of what had been billed as the last drive before lunch. Gathering my kit when the whistle went, I sprinted swiftly across the garden and established myself smugly in front of the fire, a whisky ahead of the mob. Ten minutes later, I stepped outside to investigate where the rest of the team had got to. There was a barrage of gunfire. My host had slipped in an after-thought drive at the last minute. My number had been particularly good, they all told me with relish when they clumped in. I have stuck to my leader like glue at every shoot since.

One of the paradoxes of field sports which their opponents cannot understand is that, for almost all of us, killing is far less important than companionship. One often hears friends say, 'If they banned hunting or pheasant shooting, how else would we match the pleasure of winter

Saturdays in good company?' It is never popular with hosts for guns to be caught coffee-housing between pegs when the first flush comes. Yet that is where many of us enjoy some of the season's best conversation. Sharing a rod on a salmon river, I am almost as happy wading behind a friend and chatting the morning away in the water as when I am casting for myself.

The pleasures of solitude on the hill or the river are real enough. But the opportunity to share an experience with like-minded companions is also among the sport's greatest joys. I shall never forget some summers of shooting grouse over pointers almost a quarter of century ago with two friends whom I adored and our respective wives. The novelty of the sport and the beauty of the place enthralled us. The memory created a bond which has never been broken. Sharing a day's stalking, one gets to know people very well. Long walks mean long talks, enhanced by the pauses to spy or wait whispering for a stag to stand up. In few other circumstances would one spend six or seven hours in unbroken intimacy with others. If the company is sympathetic, this doubles the pleasure of the day. Conversely, stalking all day with the wrong companions is a nightmare. I went out twenty years ago with an exceptionally crotchety and graceless retired colonel who muttered monosyllabically to the stalker as we marched, ignoring my presence until he told me to take a long shot. I missed. The grumpiness of our descent from the hill exceeded that of the morning climb.

The success of fishing parties is measured as much by the social barometer as by the tally of salmon. That is why so many Scottish fishers try to keep the same groups together year after year. It is a relief for hosts to be sure that guests rub along. They need not wait nervously for any locking of horns between new acquaintances. Come to that, for all the talk about inheriting dead men's shoes, one's best chance of receiving a first invitation to stay in a Scottish lodge comes when somebody else blots his copybook and is dropped. There are few more brutal ways to announce that a friend is no longer a friend than to leave him out of a Scottish house party after years on the ration strength.

I stay at one coveted lodge where some years ago I took over the bed of a couple whose invitations had abruptly stopped. The previous season, I was told, they had committed some enormity towards my hostess's daughter. In that house today, I refer to myself reverently as fishing the Barset-Barset Memorial rod; Barset-Barset being the name of the spurned couple. Each year, I tremble in terror at the possibility of matching their achievement, and committing some crime that gets me, in my turn, guillotined from The List.

Expensive sport makes a mockery of social scruples. 'Up the bum with rod and gun,' as a Shires hunting type used to declare gleefully, with withering scorn for those who will do anything to get on to one man's grouse moor or another's salmon river. Lots of delightful people own grouse moors. But some of Britain's leading social monsters also seem to have little trouble getting people up the hill with them if there are a hundred brace of grouse at the top of it. The owner of one famous moor is a notorious Middle East influence broker. But half the royal families of Europe, including our own, seem perfectly happy to shoot his birds and dine at his well-appointed table. Perhaps they like the colour of his eyes. But then, one of the less attractive characteristics of royal families through the ages has been their willingness to accept hospitality from almost anybody, if his cheque is good.

If I want to embarrass myself about past sporting disgraces, I think less of the days when I missed everything, than of those when I was silly enough to accept invites from people who are not really friends. Corporate sport is not always doomed to failure, because some hosts take great pains to choose jolly guests. But the odds are stacked against. Years ago, when I used to see far less sport than I do today, a friend rang up and asked, 'Do you want half a bribe?' A man with whom his firm did business had offered him two days for two rods on the Tweed. I took the fly. It was a sticky trip. Our paymaster joined us at the hotel. It was quickly obvious that he did not know one end of a rod from the other. He had fixed the expedition because he knew my friend was keen. Through the days that followed, he did not fish, but he lurked. I caught one salmon, and quite enjoyed myself. The sight of our non-fishing host jumping out from behind the hut every time we clambered up the bank, however, cast more of a damper than the drizzle.

The main trouble with corporate shooting trips, especially those involving foreign visitors, is that some of the guns have no instinct or real sympathy for the sport their bankers lay on. A few years back I took part in a promising Wiltshire partridge day with a gaggle of American tycoons. Towards the end of the morning the keeper began urging us onwards. Suddenly we were told that we had to get the big drives over by 12.30 p.m. We were hustled from peg to peg like a chain gang. Why the rush, the British contingent demanded? Two of the Americans, we were told, had suddenly decided they wanted to see a football game in Ireland that afternoon. Their jet was to be ready for take-off at 1 p.m. Maybe we had a better afternoon, because six of us shot eight guns' partridges. But somehow it was not the same. The mood of the day, which matters so much, was broken.

I have a framed photograph on the wall beside me now, as I write: it shows the team of guns assembled for a mid-morning cocktail at a day I take every season, a few miles from home. The faces are all those of men I have known and loved for years. Come pheasants or grouse in thousands, salmon in scores, friends contribute most to making a sporting day a success. Almost all of us would rather beat a hedgerow with familiar companions, than mow down flushes with a bevy of unknown bankers.

Among the many virtues of Paul Van Vlissingen's shoot at Conholt in Hampshire is the simple fact that the guns walk all day, instead of driving. All right, so there is one less morning drive. But what does that matter, compared to sustaining the vision of shooting as an open-air activity in the countryside?

One of the best things about shooters, as against fox-hunters, is that we do not talk interminably about our sport when we are not out there with a gun. The hunting frater-nity relive every fence not only at tea, but at dinner and lunch the following day. I have often thought that the only sanction likely to deter a serious animal rights supporter would be to lock him in a room with a ripe group of Shires hunting bores, and force him to listen until he recanted. Shooters, on the other hand, observe a ritual. We walk into lunch, where the assembled wives ask, 'Had a good morning?' We say, 'Marvellous, thank you,' unhesitatingly swallowing the memory of two blank drives and a complete inability to hit anything in between. Then, for the rest of lunch, we gossip about the crops, what was on telly last night, whose wife looks unlikely to stay the course past Christmas and the problems of European Monetary Union. Some of the best conversation every winter is not at poli-ticians' or publishers' tables in London but over shooting lunches.

Getting back out there afterwards in the rain can be the toughest part. We are all supposed not to mind about the weather, but of course we do, we do. A clear frosty day is worth any number of pheasants to most of us. The bag doesn't matter half as much as the setting. And anyway these days, building huge scores of pheasants comes under the heading of antisocial behaviour.

Tipping rouses fevered arguments at many shoots. Some tycoons believe that if they do not give keepers extravagant handouts they will be thought to have let the side down. Venerable pillars of the peerage rarely make this mistake. If anything, they have to be shaken pretty hard to get anything out of them at all. But I have been at a few days at which the proposed tip for the keeper seemed so absurd – however big the bag – that I made my own arbitrary public spending cut. I like the legendary response of an outraged gun to an industrialist host who proposed a three-figure *pourboire*: 'I want to tip the man, not **** him.' It seems reasonable to ratchet a contribution up or down according to whether one's own experience of the day has been good or bad. A tip is intended as a personal gesture to the keeper, not a mass levy towards the thatching of his roof.

But where should we all be without these ridiculous social dilemmas and the jolly debate which they provoke at so many shooting lunches? Winston Churchill's definition of a gentleman was 'someone who is only rude intentionally'. Many of us, I am afraid, get it wrong accidentally too often to be able to play high hat towards those who err as a matter of policy.

5

Jolly Boating Weather

I HAVE ALWAYS resisted *Three Men in a Boat*. It is a coy, mannered Victorian romp in the fashion of the period – my own grandfather published many essays of the same provenance, even if his never attained Jerome's classic status. Middle-class late Victorians had little to trouble them, and much of their comic literature made heavy weather of trifles. The elephantine set pieces of *Three Men in a Boat* have as much appeal for me as Charlie Chaplin films. How could any countryman appreciate a writer who saddled a dog with a name like Montmorency?

By now, I have lost the sympathy of at least half my

readers, evenly divided between those who adore Jerome K. Jerome and those who think Chaplin funny. But my point is that, while I have always been up for a bit of messing about in boats, I have avoided the genteel reaches of the Thames like the plague unless a punt and a fantastically pretty girl have been involved. There was that day when I went punting with a mate and his girlfriend, and after we had disembarked to pull the punt over some rollers, she got in and I got in, and I decided the afternoon would be brighter and merrier with just the two of us, and poled off . . . But never mind, that is another story and not a madly creditable one. Sufficient to say that I had not ventured on to the Thames for more than twenty years, until one weekend when fishing looked unpromising, and I had two large sons to amuse.

Although I have lived not far from the river for much of my life, there are great tracts of it which I have never explored. On a whim, I told the crew that we were going boating for the weekend. On Friday afternoon we collected our rented cruiser from Eynsham, a few miles above Oxford, and set off downstream with ample provisions, no straw hats or banjoleles, and a dog sensibly named Paddy.

The Hastings family are veterans of many an expedition through the canals of France and Shropshire. We have been involved in most nautical activities, including piracy. That is to say, arriving as scheduled at a Brittany canal basin one evening, we found the whole place closed and locked for the weekend. Enraged and frustrated, we simply broke into our destined boat and sailed away. I will not bore you with details of the recriminations which pursued us to Nantes and beyond. I will also pass over the holiday on which I thought it would be amusing to cruise a stretch of the Canal de Bretagne which involved covering ninety-two locks in a week, an experience which caused the rest of the family to send me to Coventry for some days afterwards.

Sufficient to say that when we set off down the Thames, we thought we knew about inland cruisers. That day in Oxfordshire we listened impatiently to the careful technical instructions we were given about driving, maintenance, rules of the road and so on. Silly us. The odd thing is that even after an interval of a year or two, one forgets a lot of the custom and practice. I was suitably grateful, afterwards, that I had been talked through all the stuff about diesel pre-heating and turning on the cooker, otherwise we would still be adrift somewhere north of Abingdon.

Holiday cruisers are wonderfully built to be handled by idiots, and of course most of them are. At our first lock, I began to realize how much I had forgotten about the need to understeer. But Thames lock-keepers are used to people like us. Our man consoled me about the difficulty of steering into a stiff breeze, told my sons how to fix a running mooring, and decanted us six or eight feet downhill. We started to enjoy ourselves.

Much of the charm of boating is that one sees even a familiar landscape from a new perspective. First, there were the flat, twisting empty reaches of the river above Oxford, where Paddy raced along the bank beside us, ignoring the protests of great flocks of swans and geese. We passed through Eynsham and Godstow, with thirty-year-old memories of happy hours at The Trout, and dropped down into the backstreets of Oxford sitting in the stern with a mug of tea.

The imposing frontage of college boathouses fell behind, and the lovely locks at Iffley and Sandford. We entered a long stretch of Thames wilderness, of which I savoured every mile. Knowing that above the river, new housing estates and dual carriageways crowd the horizon in every direction, it is enchanting to perceive how the river-bank has, to a remarkable extent, preserved its virginity. We chugged onwards amidst great tracts of rushes and ducks, marvelling at the emptiness of the vista.

That night we moored by a wood, without a sign of human life in any direction. I cooked for the crew without much audible complaint about the fare, triumphed at Scrabble and slept in my clothes, a pastime I am getting a bit old for.

Oh yes, you will expect to hear that something went wrong. I shall indulge you modestly. The only unhappy member of this party was Paddy, who detested the boat from start to finish. Early in the evening, he curled up on the bank. At bedtime, I asked my elder son to bring him back aboard. From the cabin, I heard much cursing and struggling ashore, culminating in an abrupt splash and even worse language. Paddy, it seemed, had resisted the press gang with vigour. He attempted escape into the wood with such determination that my son sampled the Thames up to the waist. No, he did not have a change of clothes aboard. Paddy eventually rejoined us after my intervention, at a cost of only one leg and two shoes immersed. Jerome K. Jerome would have written three pages about this episode. Not being a Victorian, I shall simply report that I told my son to stop moaning and think of England, which he did.

A light rain began to fall. I remembered a dreadful day on the Normandy canal, when I had driven ahead of our craft, to leave a car. I then bicycled back along the tow path to a riverside rendezvous. Torrential rain descended in sheets. I waited two hours at the appointed lock. The head of the family was in charge of the boat. She took one look at the mudsoaked object standing waiting and called from midstream, 'If you think you are coming aboard here like that, you are not!' I begged. I pleaded. I remember thinking:

thank the Lord my staff at the *Daily Telegraph* can't see this pitiable humiliation. Finally, after desperate imprecations and the intercession of my children, I stripped to my underpants, washed the bike in the canal, and was grudgingly allowed to crawl aboard. Below Abingdon, I reminded the children to be suitably grateful they were not required to walk the plank on this occasion.

I am intrigued by the social etiquette of the Thames. Fellow weekend sailors in rented cruisers wave heartily to each other, saluting mutual ignorance and incompetence. Narrow-boat dwellers, a tribe of their own, affect disdain. The serious snobs, however, are the gin-palace sailors. These are the men and women, mostly middle-aged (empty nesters, as we sociologists call them), who advance upriver in great glistening three-deckers like Surbiton wedding cakes, bursting with brass gadgets and designer fabrics in the lounge. The helmsmen, superb in their little blue yachting caps, scorn to notice rented cruisers any more than do their pekes, reposing at stately ease on their dashboards.

Only at the locks do these floating Pooters spring to life. Their wives, clutching at perfectly manicured Manila ropes, shriek rape at the touch of a glancing stern. That they should be so lucky. I gave my sons a noisy lecture about the imposing radar arrays of these top-heavy vessels, towering above the cockpits. 'Those are in case they lose their way to Abingdon.' What a gang.

No, really, we loved the whole business. I must confess that at Wallingford we cheated and drove home in the car I had prudently parked the day before. After a bath and ten or twelve hours sleep in a bed, my team was bursting to be back on the river (Paddy was unable to express an audible opinion). But we were pitifully grateful for that interlude in beds, even though the boat had a very natty shower and sheets and duvets.

We returned upriver in bright sunshine, gazing upon the Thames at its best. If I drive around Abingdon or the back passages of Oxford in a car, it is unlikely that I shall think beautiful thoughts. But the river is still marvellously preserved. I love the lock-keepers in their absurd sea-going uniforms. Most of them preserve their welcome and sense of humour amazingly well, given the daily procession of fools like us they have to deal with.

Each great weir or arched stone bridge charms a new spectator, and the wildlife is rich and varied. We cooked bacon and eggs on Monday morning and ate them sitting at the back of the open cockpit in the misty sunshine, puttering back towards Godstow amid dinghies and longboats.

My affection and respect for the life of the river grew with the miles we covered: past the old Victorian boat-houses, the rich men's bijoux residences with immaculately mown grass running down to the waterside. I felt a glow of goodwill towards them all; and maybe even, in the end, towards that old *poseur* Jerome K. Jerome.

6

ROUGH AND FUMBLE

ONE OF MY happiest days' shooting last season happened on 1 February. At the invitation of a kind neighbour, I took a couple of boys to join his family walking the water meadows half a mile or so below my house. We lined out behind a few questing dogs and passed the morning flushing fugitive pheasants, of which two out of three survived the erratic barrage.

Why don't some of us do this more often? Why is rough-shooting a relatively neglected sport in many parts of the country and driven shoots achieve a monopoly? Much of the answer is that the demand for driven shooting is so great that in the South of England almost every acre is given up to formal arrangements which leave little scope for freelances to mess around. This is a pity, especially for children. As a teenager, I was happy to cycle anywhere a neighbouring farmer would let me walk the hedges of his rolling downs. Even in my early twenties, I relied for much of my shooting on a neighbour who gave me free run over 200-odd acres of boarding-school grounds, including some good spinneys. In those days, I didn't have a dog of my own. I borrowed my father's batty old spaniel for flushing purposes. When it came to retrieving a long runner, I often ended up bounding on all fours through the undergrowth myself. Observers remarked that they didn't think much of my nose and suspected me of having a hard mouth.

A few years later, I owned a labrador but still didn't get many driven days. I made the most of walking-up miles of Leicestershire hedges. The dog had a great nose but no brakes. When he winded a pheasant and started cantering in pursuit, my only hope of a shot was to race after him like a demon, in order to be somewhere near the scene of the crime when he eventually put up the bird. At the end of a couple of hours, I was happy to go home with one in the bag, thrilled to take a brace. It was all very small beer, but I loved it. Instinctively, I felt this was the purest form of shooting. Could the Americans be on the mark when they call any activity involving a dog, a man and a bird 'hunting'? I could argue all night with an 'anti' about the merits of this kind of shooting. Why should it be that my throat gets a trifle drier when it comes to explaining the intellectual arguments in favour of eight men standing still all day while others hunt up the game for them?

It is sometimes forgotten just how passionately many sportsmen opposed driven shooting – the *battue*, as it was called – on its introduction to England in the late nineteenth century. My own shelves contain many books which include contemporary denunciations. 'Since its introduction into England, *battue* shooting has been exposed to constant and severe criticism,' wrote Ralph Nevill in 1910, 'accounts of the vast quantities of game slaughtered making much impression upon sensitive minds.'

Nevill quoted one Victorian critic who wrote, 'Of all the un-Englishmanlike, unsportsmanlike practices which I have witnessed in the field, that called the *battue* is the most offensive to a real sportsman; and the most strenuous defender of it can only place it one degree beyond shooting rooks in a rookery.'

'Stonehenge', the famous editor of the *Field*, wrote with withering scorn of driven shooting in 1875. 'None but men of large means, and in possession of extensive coverts, can indulge in this amusement . . . in this instance power has been abused, and instead of promoting sport, it has totally destroyed it. No one can deny the fitness of the pheasant for affording gratification to the good sportsman, if the bird is fairly found, put up, and shot; but as well might "mobbing" a fox be called fox-hunting, as a *battue* be considered genuine pheasant shooting.'

In some respects our forefathers were more cruel than ourselves. Pierce Egan suggested in 1844 that 'in order to acquire the art of shooting flying, many young sportsmen are advised to shoot at swallows . . . We will venture to recommend another mode . . . this is, by putting small pieces of white paper round the necks of sparrows, then throwing a single bird into the air; the shooter may deliberately take his aim; by this device, the flight of the bird is rendered less rapid and more regular, and at the same time presents a much better mark for practice. It also affords an excellent diversion in seasons when game cannot be pursued, or in wet weather, from underneath the shelter of a shed, or a barn door. Some of the finest shots in England have been perfected by this mode.'

Yet the same men who could amuse themselves in this style, so repugnant to modern taste, recoiled from shooting pheasants which were driven over their heads without exertion on the part of anyone save the birds. I can understand how those Victorian sportsmen felt, in the days when rough-shooting was to be had more or less for the asking all over Britain. The pheasant was still perceived as a rare and special delicacy, commanding thirty shillings a brace from the game dealers – in real money about what we might pay for caviar today.

True sportsmen devoted themselves chiefly to the pursuit of wild grey partridges, of which there were abundant coveys on almost every stubble in the kingdom – some of them within a brisk walk of the capital. A party of guns killed ten brace of partridges on a September morning on Wimbledon Common as late as 1842, and until a few years earlier there was an annual ritual march out of London on 1st September, to pursue partridges in the wilds of Hackney, Islington, Clapham and the Lambeth Marshes. Wary countrymen drove off their pigs, cows and poultry in advance of the invasion of these prodigously dangerous cockney sportsmen, but that did not save the watchman's dog at Middlesex Hospital, which was killed by three shooters in mistake for a greyleg on a dawn patrol in 1795.

Those confrontations between very rough shooters and countrymen produced some of the early archetypal humour of a genre which persists to this day:

Cockney sportsman to yokel, as he peers over hedge in search of supposedly shot bird: 'I say, you have not seen a partridge fall this way, have you?'

Yokel: 'Not the very smallest one, sir.'

Sportsman: 'It is very odd, for I certainly saw some of the feathers fly.'

Yokel: 'Oh! I saw them too, and they flew so well they carried the flesh with them.'

In grander sporting circles, some of those pre-*battue* shooters managed to make impressive bags, even over dogs. Coke of Norfolk and a party at Holkham in 1811 accounted for 264 pheasants, 314 partridges, 29 woodcock, 283 hares, 46 snipe, 371 rabbits – not a bad score for men shooting with flintlock guns.

In the early nineteenth century when agricultural prices were soaring during the Napoleonic wars, some landowners convinced themselves that game was a damaging embarrassment on their estates, because of the quantities of corn consumed by pheasants and hares. In 1812, a group of landowners in Staffordshire held a meeting at which they agreed to try to kill off all the game and vermin on their acres. About the same time, the *Kent Gazette* published an extraordinary advertisement headed: 'A general invitation to *qualified gentlemen* – the interests of agriculture in this manor of Dennie in the parishes of Chilham and Molash, being much injured by the great numbers of hares, pheasants and rabbits, the proprietor feels the necessity of giving a general invitation to *qualified gentlemen* to sport at their pleasure.' It would be naive to hope for any repetition today of that wonderful advertisement (which even offered free bed and board). But how nice it would be if there were more farmers willing to let rough-shooting for a modest rent, instead of a tariff based upon the assumption of big shots and big bags.

Most of us find driven-game shooting enjoyable, especially socially, but we also recognize that something is lost from sport when one is called upon for no physical effort save that of firing a shotgun again and again. Last season, I noticed a grandee at the end of a massively killing drive, who simply handed the gun to his loader and waddled away to the vehicles. He believed that it was not a job for a sporting gent to bother to bend down and pick up birds. Yet some of us enjoy nothing more than spending twenty minutes looking for a difficult runner, especially on a grouse moor.

Of course when it comes to testing marksmanship, an away bird flushed at one's feet is generally an easier shot than a high driven pheasant. But so often out walking, one is raising the gun to a long, low, crossing bird sneaking out of a hedge, which can be as tough a target as anything Castle Hill produces. Shooting from a peg, one is poised and ready, handling a gun under almost ideal conditions. When walking, by contrast, a bird always gets up while one is stuck with a leg in a fence, the gamebag on the wrong shoulder or the gun empty for crossing a ditch. That is called luck, and thus – to most of us – sport.

Dogs adore rough-shooting. We know that letting them roam in front of a line is not good for discipline. But what a pleasure it is to send Ponto to pick up without having to enter a steeplechase against an aggressive picker-up behind the line. At most shoots these days, the guns are given a little homily at the start: no ground game, no wild partridges, no woodcock or whatever. This is all perfectly sensible, but it makes the contrast all the more fun on a Heinz 57-varieties outing. A friend in Northumberland has access to a few hundred acres of rough moorland where on a September day one can reasonably expect to shoot the odd grouse, blackcock, partridge, woodcock, snipe, hare, rabbit or pigeon. Most of the sport hinges upon elaborate sweeps, wherein a couple of guns drive a car six hundred yards, dismount and take cover in the peat hags. The rest then walk the moor towards them. There are usually a few bangs before the teams meet for recriminations:

'Didn't you hear me shout about that covey on the right?'

'You realize two blackcock went *straight* over your head while you were gazing at the bloody wild flowers?'

'When I say "Go and stand a hundred yards east of the third fence post beyond the scree," I *don't* mean fifty yards west.'

And so on, and so on. Nobody really minds at all. In jolly company, on a sunny day amid the drystone walls, scrub and big horizons, it is bliss, except on the rare occasions when somebody shoots too much and you are stuck with the gamebag. God, what a gamebag can weigh on a hot day, the burden increasing incrementally by about a third for every ten years of the bearer's age.

A few years ago in Spain I picked up an accessory few people use in Britain, but just about everyone carries on the Continent: a shotgun sling which slips on to the barrel and small of the butt. This can be a great help on a rough day, along with a few large teenagers to carry the lunch and a grapnel for my inexhaustible dog. I have used the same old Webley & Scott boxlock for rough-shooting since my father gave it to me thirty-five years ago. Like most of my kind, I dress for rough-shooting as if for the seedier sort of tramp's funeral. I come home exhausted, having fired a paltry handful of cartridges that would not keep your Hampshire toff amused for more than three minutes on a 'proper' day. But cross my heart, it's enough for me.

7

BATS AND BELFRIES

THE OTHER DAY, one of the foremost of the Great and Good described to me a university luncheon at which the wife of a vastly rich benefactor suddenly turned to him and enquired earnestly, 'Don't you agree that this meal would be *infinitely* more rewarding if Our Saviour himself was in our midst?'

Her neighbour mused in silence over the appropriate answer to that one and retired to the pavilion stumped. I told the story to a mutual friend. He said that he hesitated to cap it, but could not help recalling an occasion on which he congratulated the same woman on leading in a rather handy 25–1 winner at Kempton. 'He did not do it for *us*,' she replied sombrely. 'He did it *for Jesus*.'

Now, don't think I am being blasphemous here. I am merely reflecting upon eccentricity, and the question of when it stops charming and becomes a trifle embarrassing. I know what I am talking about, because my own family has been pretty well endowed with eccentrics or – let us call a spade a shovel – with characters thought by all who knew them to be several stitches short of a blanket. Looking through some of my family's nineteenth-century correspondence recently, I was struck by how much of it was preoccupied with the state of the writers' immortal souls – this applied even to letters to fourteen-year-old Hastingses at unspeakably austere boarding schools. Religion was a family obsession, from which I am grateful that we seem recovered today. In recent years, however, while my relations may have stopped going on about God, they have indulged some fairly outlandish habits, of which my father's excesses with firearms were at the lower end of the scale. Unkind people suggest that I take after Father, but their jibes reflect a pathetic lack of appreciation of individuality. Why shouldn't one cook a fox for a local Master? If you get the marinade right, it is a vast improvement on the fare he gets at home.

Eccentrics may grow no thicker in the country than in London, but they stick out more, as Squire Mytton could have testified. I remember a visit to the home of a charming but frankly batty divorcee. We hove up to a vast pile where the central heating had been turned off years ago. Miss Havisham would have been impressed by the rich coating of dust on every Sèvres plate in the drawing room. With difficulty a half-empty half-bott of whisky was found, to give us a drink.

Dinner started inauspiciously, with some sort of vegetarian spinach soufflé, which I skipped in the hope of better things to come. Then dawned the creeping perception that there would be no further things to come, better or otherwise, save a discussion on the importance of the stars in regulating our lives. Oddly enough, even a decade later I don't think our hostess has remarried, though that evening I would have welcomed an invitation to share her bed, merely for a little warmth.

I won't start talking about eccentrics in Ireland, because a host of contenders would be so offended by being left off the wine list. Many Irishmen spend the daylight hours stalking the hedgerows in search of either game or a cocktail, while many of their women seem bemused to understand how the husbands whom they met as dashing young Irish Guards officers at St James's have been transformed a generation later into misogynistic recluses whose idea of a good crack is a season ticket to the Owners' and Trainers' bar at Leopardstown.

Norfolk harbours more than its share of English eccentricity. Incest has always been the nearest thing the county can offer to an indoor pastime. One meets so few new people, y'know. There is still a remarkable concentration of batty squires living in great East Anglian barracks from which they venture out only to visit the pheasants or stalk a goose behind the sea wall.

For connoisseurs of rural battiness, Mytton remains the icon, with his midnight shooting expeditions in the snow in his nightshirt, loose bears in the house, and general determination to prevent tedium gaining command of his life. He achieved immortality with his response to a passenger he was driving, who remarked complacently that he had never been in an accident. 'Never been upturned in a gig? What a damn dull fellow you must be!' exploded the Squire, whipping the horse into a ditch.

Enoch Powell, a considerable eccentric in his own right, borrowed the line when he turned over a three-tonner in the North African desert in 1943. I have not forgotten an occasion when Powell came to lunch with us at the *Daily Telegraph* half a century later and proved in awkward and unresponsive mood. In desperation, I tried to turn the conversation to AIDS, then as now hogging the headlines.

Powell fixed me with his glittering Ancient Mariner's eye, and delivered a withering put down: '*Mr* Editor! *Mr* Editor! When one has attained the age of seventy-nine, the prospect of death from a sexually transmitted disease appears *remarkably* remote.'

Some exceptionally good-natured friends of mine some years ago took pity on a family of newcomers to their village, who seemed to be having trouble getting to know people. The new couple, who boasted some social pretension, duly turned up for dinner and drank in the drawing room for half an hour, before the husband sprang to his feet without explanation, marched out, and was heard starting his car and driving away. 'I'm *so* sorry,' said his wife, 'but he *simply* felt he couldn't stand your friends a minute longer.' Their hostess was suitably amazed by this episode, no less so when the wife of this epic boor accosted her on the school run a day or two later. She was rash enough to imagine an apology was imminent. Not quite. '*Such* a shame about the other night,' said the wife in a shameless echo of her refrain before dinner, 'but I'm afraid poor David just couldn't *bear* your other guests.' Mad, or just bad?

Not a few perfectly sane people cultivate mild eccentricities in the belief that these will enhance their image – shooting in a long overcoat and bush hat, eating raw grouse on the moor, peppering overhead hot-air balloons and suchlike. The trouble is, these types are prone to lose the plot about whether they are really eccentric or just pretending to be. I have always been deeply fond of a landowning friend who is warm-hearted, generous and prone to gestures which astonish those who don't know his little ways. Twenty years ago he invited me to shoot at a field trial on his land. On arrival, he introduced us to a fellow gun whom he said had never shot before but was tremendously keen to get going. Somebody murmured a word of doubt about whether this was the right occasion for an armed debut, airily waved aside by our host. The reservations were revived half an hour later, however, when we heard an explosion and a canine howl on the other side of a spinney. The inevitable had happened. The novice had mistaken a spaniel for a rabbit. A priceless four-legged star had to be removed in a van with sirens screaming, emergency drips dripping, oxygen tents in waiting.

As you might imagine, this mishap cast a shadow over the rest of the proceedings. Every time a gun was raised thereafter, handlers threw themselves protectively in front of their beloved Towsers, fears only slightly alleviated by a message from Emergency Ward 10 that the casualty was expected to pull through. Our host was the only one happily oblivious of the atmosphere. At the close of play, while prize-giving was being arranged, he darted over to our lonely little group and remarked confidentially, 'There's a special prize for "Guns' choice of dog of the day". Do you think we should give it to the dog that was shot?'

As late as the beginning of the nineteenth century, there was a convention that military men enjoyed wide-ranging freedom to help themselves to a little rough-shooting in the woods around their garrison towns. But as the ownership of sporting rights became more rigorously asserted, bitter controversies erupted about military poaching. On taking over his inheritance, a young peer was enraged to find that a captain of infantry from the nearby garrison was hunting partridges through his turnips without so much as a by-your-leave, the officer having been in the habit of supposing that no such leave was necessary. His lordship ordered his keeper to shoot the captain's dogs on sight. When the keeper finally caught up with the unwanted guest and reported his orders, the captain coolly told him to shoot the pointer on the right first.

The moment the keeper fired, the officer raised his own gun. He felled the keeper's pony in its tracks. 'Now this is horse for dog,' said the captain contemptuously. 'Fire again, and it shall be man for dog. Otherwise go home and tell your master that if he crosses my path in town or country, I shall horsewhip him back to his own front door.' Hard times, hard times.

Like most eccentrics, my own father was a connoisseur of others. A lifelong chum, named Pat Murray, who founded the Museum of Childhood in Edinburgh, lived in unspeakable squalor in a flat so densely crowded with books and a fabulous collection of model soldiers that visitors were invited to compete to find the bed. Another friend, Hugh Pollard, spent his youth as a Black and Tan and helped to smuggle Franco into Spain at the outset of the Civil War before settling down to write his great *History of Firearms*. As a child, I was much impressed by Hugh's dislike of leaving any gun around the house unloaded. He argued that one never knew when it might be needed.

At root, eccentricity only means behaving in a way we're not used to. One man's eccentric is another man's soulmate. It is much easier to be eccentric if you are rich, because you do not need to retain the good opinion of an employer, as Paul Getty might testify. You can also get away with a lot if you are called Churchill rather than Smith. Wasn't it Randolph who peed in the dining-room fireplace at the Beefsteak Club? In modern times I doubt whether the members would still swallow these little whims, but you can do your bit for the tradition. I took a very urban friend of mine to a St James's dining club a few months ago. Late in the evening he recoiled in terror when three young cavalry officers in the corner sprang to their feet shouting in unison, 'Prepare to mount!' I calmed my friend with the assurance that this was perfectly normal. 'Compared to what?' he demanded. Well – Squire Mytton, for one.

8

Ripples on a Chalk Stream

It is sometimes thought mere snobbery to suggest that casting a dry fly on a chalk stream is the most challenging form of sport. The truth is more complicated. There are many southern rivers where even a moderate fisher can catch a few reared trout with one of the great panacea flies – a Hawthorn early in, a Grey Wulff, a pheasant-tail nymph in August. In recent years, I have fulfilled a lasting ambition, to live within a few hundred yards of the Kennet, where I can wander down for a couple of hours any time when conditions are promising. I don't much mind whether I catch fish, but I love to walk the river-bank among the wild flowers and the duck, the water rats and willows.

Any dry fly is a more pleasing lure than the hairy monsters deployed by anglers for still-water wet-fly fishing. I am conscious, however, that even after a good few years fishing, I have failed to make the most of the chalk stream, because I have never got to grips with its entomology. J. W. Dunne put it well, in his 1924 classic *Sunshine and the Dry Fly*: 'The love of Nature which the fly-fisherman may enlist to his advantage,' he says, 'covers an area a hundred times greater, and a thousand times richer, than are those which lie open to, for example, the votaries of bait and minnow.'

He meant, of course, that in order to catch a selectively feeding trout with a fly, he himself went to extraordinary lengths to match the artificial perfectly with the natural prey. Like every great fisherman, Dunne made himself a master of the insect life of the river-bank, and derived supreme pleasure from discovering by observation what trout were feeding upon. 'The appeal of a sport – being simply an appeal to age-old inherited instincts – is never experienced in its full perfection unless there is involved some call upon that craft of the wilderness, that faculty of appreciating the ways of bird and beast, the acquirement of which was, through countless centuries, the one great primary interest of primitive man.'

The approach of Dunne and his peers makes dry-fly fishing at its higher levels a much more profound activity than shooting. It is a pleasure to watch an elegant shot consistently hit difficult pheasants. But the man with the gun, however accomplished, need not call upon much knowledge of nature to do the business. He requires only physical coordination and some practice. The serious dry-fly fisherman draws upon a well of study and experience matched only by that of a great professional huntsman.

Dear old G. E. M. Skues, master of the Itchen and many other rivers besides, recommended every fisherman to travel with his own marrow-scoop, to explore the stomach of the first trout he catches. Skues went further: 'In July 1908 I caught an Itchen fish one afternoon, and on examining his mouth found a dark olive nymph. My fly dressing materials were with me, and I found I had a seal's fur which, with a small admixture of bear's hair, dark brown and woolly, from close to the skin, enabled me to reproduce exactly the colours of the natural insect.' Those of us who, in similar circumstances, merely make a ten-minute dash for the fly boxes of Roxtons in Hungerford, blush in shame.

Yet, for all one's admiration of those old masters, it is sometimes hard not to flinch at the obsessiveness of their approach. Skues was not merely a fisherman but a killer, who delighted in taking four brace from a stream in an afternoon and went back for more. Given that he roamed with his rod as far afield as Norway, Normandy and Bavaria, it is scarcely surprising that there are not many wild fish left in the rivers covered by himself and his kind. They seemed to have room in their lives for nothing, absolutely nothing, save the capture of trout. 'I thought myself lucky in that during a holiday on the Itchen in the last week of August 1914, I had a little moonlight on this interesting subject,' observed Skues. Yes, man, but did you not for a moment notice that at the same hour you were single-mindedly addressing Itchen fish, the fortunes of the world hung poised on the battlefields of France, where at that moment Allied armies stood with their backs against the wall?

I am afraid we know the answer to that question, because Skues recorded in 1916: 'Saturday, July 1, was a mixed bag of a day. Fine, warm, morning, but windy; afternoon, windy and cold with a fine drizzle after five o'clock.' That formidable angler got on the water at 7 a.m. with his beloved cane Leonard, and went home the same evening content with 7½ brace and the success of another wet-fly experiment, apparently oblivious then or later of the fact that this was the first day of the Battle of the Somme, on which 60,000 Englishmen fell, almost within earshot of Skues' river.

For those great fishermen, catching trout was not a mere recreation, it was the passion of their lives. They knew far more than most of us, and they cared more. Their public controversies – for example, that of Skues and his enemies about the ethics of nymphing – were conducted with a bitterness that is hard to imagine being matched today, whatever the disagreements between different schools of fishermen.

The little London solicitor and his *confrères* rose, as if to the mayfly, in their public disgust towards a certain Professor Ludwig Edinger, who wrote an article for the *Field* before the First World War, under the heading 'Fish and Free Will'. In a wonderful outbreak of German sophistry, the Professor declared that the action of a trout in taking a fly is an involuntary reflex action, that the creature's brain renders it incapable of an act of choice. The question of whether it does or does not accept the lure, he said, is determined only by whether the stimulus is adequate and the degree of excitability of the nerve centre sufficient. The fish's choice 'is none, when the temptation is irresistible'.

Now, you or I reading this sort of thing would merely shrug sardonically that one might say the same about girls, and the Professor's sage advice is about as much practical use in dealing with them. But for Edwardian anglers, Edinger's contention seemed to imply that they were wasting their time, and that one dun was not much different from another. Here was heresy.

They would probably think it equally heretical to observe me on a fine May afternoon, my rod lying idle by my side as I let half an hour slip by, gazing fascinated upon the fast water racing through a Kennet sluice gate. I like to catch a trout or two, but I feel not the slightest interest in netting $7^{1}/_{2}$ brace on a day when they are rising freely. The river-bank offers so many pleasures beyond those merely of catching fish. One evening last season, I was lucky enough to be a guest on one of the noblest and most famous stretches of the Test. I caught a couple of monsters, one over 5lb. I enjoyed myself, but I was not persuaded that I had done anything very clever. That water was stocked to the gills with immense trout, slashing the surface as they rose to sedges. The setting, the charm of watching gin-clear water run over gravel and gently curvetting weed while the cows grazed against the flat horizon, meant as much to me as anything in the net. As my fishing experience grows, I want to learn as Dunne and Skues learnt – but for the pleasure of gaining a tiny fraction of their vast knowledge of Nature, rather than to match their fantastic catches.

9

HOUSE GUESTS

FOR OBVIOUS REASONS, to do with gardens, picnics and long sunny days, normal people who want to entertain friends for the weekend arrange dates in the summer months. It is one of the peculiarities of field sports that their followers usually conduct the migratory cycle to each other's houses between October and the beginning of February. This is less convenient for consorts not doing the shooting or hunting. In early December, what is a hostess supposed to do with a grumpy female guest who declares that she is damned if she is going to stand all day watching her expletive-deleted husband missing chickens or falling in ditches? In the end, the guest leans against the Aga all day discussing her crumbling marriage while the chatelaine struggles to prepare dinner for ten. Some hostesses offer impassioned recommendations that tiresome visitors simply *must* call upon that wonderful local antiques shop only thiry miles away. The most desperate are said to offer faint-hearted visitors a cash subsidy to stay out of the house between ten and four on Saturday.

Surtees remarked that rural social life is conducted on the debtor and creditor principle. It is a mortal insult to accept a neighbour's invitation to dinner and decline to return it. In August, as soon as it is known that the Shooter-Joneses are coming for the weekend in November, the struggle begins to decide which neighbours to ask with them on Saturday night. This is especially testing if you live in one of Britain's remoter corners and entertain dedicated urbanites. I would be stretching a point to call myself more than half rural, but I hope I am not as difficult to amuse as Londoners whose Mercedes station wagons have not seen mud since the same weekend last year. As a topic of conversation, four tons an acre does not possess much magic if you conduct your own husbandry in Clapham. When I lived in Northamptonshire, a ruthlessly frank, urban guest once rang ahead and said that he would double the generosity of his weekend present if he could be spared a dinner party on Saturday night. We succumbed weakly. Perhaps one should do so more often.

I tremble about arriving at houses where I only remember on the gravel outside on Friday night that somebody else will be unpacking my case. By then it is too late to do anything about last weekend's rather scruffy shooting stockings rolled up in a bundle in my case with a ragged sweater and a few pheasant feathers. Staying in Angus a while ago, I found myself in a dinner jacket and bare feet, conducting humiliating negotiations with the host's domestic staff for the liberation of my black socks so that I could go down to dinner. They had been removed for washing that morning, on the assumption that no gentleman would wear the same socks two nights running.

It is essential for a guest to know how much staying power will be expected on Saturday night. Some houses, which I enjoy more as I get older, pull the shutters down at eleven. However, few go to the same lengths as a neighbouring Shires family, to whom we drove for our first visit one Saturday night many years ago, to make up the numbers with their house party. At 10.45 p.m., our host advanced towards us with a theatrical glance at his watch and a skeletal smile. 'We do go to bed *frightfully* early here,' he announced. Once a visitor had got used to this abrupt and rigorous social regime one recognized its merits.

By contrast, when we lived in Ireland, there was a house in the neighbourhood to which nobody was invited a second time if they flagged before 3 a.m., a pretty debilitating business for dinner guests who had been out all day and possessed no staff of their own. After we moved back to England, we were invited to stay the weekend at the house. We learnt the secret. Nobody got up in the morning before ten. After hunting, an army of flunkies did the dirty work while the household retired to bed at four and did not surface again until nine. If you live like that, you can be incredibly jolly in the small hours.

I enjoy houses where the ritual has been abolished of men staying alone in the dining room after dinner. Not a lot of people drink port any more, and there is a modest but growing minority culture of Englishmen, even in rural circles, who enjoy the society of women. Perhaps it is a reflection on the company I keep that it is years since I heard even a very bad dirty story at the table after dinner.

There is usually desultory political speculation and a little chat about how business is going, until a decent interval has elapsed and the men can decamp to the drawing room. Nobody who has once played bridge with me repeats the error.

A plague on diligent hostesses who try to tell everybody with whom they are to sit after dinner. By that stage of the evening almost everybody knows exactly whom they want to seek out and, more important, whom they want to avoid. If one gets a bad draw, one can wage conversational guerrilla warfare by providing a twenty-minute answer to the question, 'How did the shooting go?' which usually provokes a dash for the loo midway through a description of the third drive. With luck, by 10.30 it will anyway be time for that matchless experience, bed.

In most houses where there isn't a cast of thousands to clear up after dinner on Saturday, right-thinking hosts shoo their guests upstairs so that they can sort out the shambles in peace and avoid being detected emptying wine glasses back into bottles. It is also nice for visitors to be spared the marital recriminations inseparable from dinner parties: 'Why did you ignore poor Julia right through until the coffee?', 'What were you thinking of, telling Jane that horse Peter is selling has killed someone? Let her find out for herself. Anyway it was ages ago,' and so on.

Self-respecting weekend guests should leave on Sunday morning. Every possible avenue of conversation has been exhausted. Most people with work to do on Monday yearn for a breather before the week starts. The garden at home howls for Sunday-afternoon attention.

As the guests drive away, parallel post-mortems get under way in the abandoned sitting room, and in the departing car.

'You shouldn't have mentioned schools. It was very

unkind of you to tell them what a good reputation Giggles-
wick has these days.'

'Why won't you listen when I tell you that cooks get
prizes for attainment not effort?'

'I don't mind their bloody dog sleeping in the bedroom,
but on the bed, after shooting . . .'

'You should know better than to start talking about
Lloyd's when they've got that shooting print over the fireplace where the Ben Marshall used to be.'

I like to think that I am reasonably efficient, but I have
a shocking reputation for leaving property behind in other
people's houses. Hosts are entitled to regard caps and
shooting sticks as spoils of war. But ear defenders are so
expensive that one must get them back somehow. Perhaps
I should leave behind a large stamped and self-addressed
jiffy bag in any house I visit, though that would scarcely
have coped with the disaster a year or two ago. I slipped
away home early on Sunday morning, and posted a dutiful
thank-you letter in which I congratulated myself on having,
for once, failed to leave anything behind. I then discovered
that I had abandoned my suitcase on my host's drive. Oh
well, it gave them something to talk about.

Perhaps the greatest single change to overtake country
life in the past fifty years is that it has become comfortable.
In former times, however grand a host and however large
his house, few guests could count on a hot bath and even
fewer on a warm room, as James Lees-Milne's splendid
diaries testify. Jokes were legion about the hideous suffer-
ings inseparable from discomforts of country-house or, worse
still, of cottage weekends. Evelyn Waugh wrote vividly
about John Beaver's ghastly experience at Hatton in *A
Handful of Dust*, only marginally redeemed by Beaver's later
seduction by his hostess. In the days before the motor car
became available to fox-hunters, being driven ten miles to

a meet in an unheated wagonette was the only alternative
to a long, hard hack. Dukes suffered almost as much getting
up to grouse moors or deer forests as did commoners. Until
recently, the difficulty of buying a decent vegetable outside
a city was a standing joke. Food in most houses was awful
because there were far more bad cooks than good ones.

Today, when it is a cliché to complain relentlessly about
how civilization is collapsing around us, country dwellers
have never had it so good. We can buy really good food
and enjoy much higher standards of cooking; long-distance
telephones work perfectly; few houses dare threaten guests
with the lack of a hot bath and a warm room. Every country
magazine peddles advertisements for rural luxuries: thermal
underwear and electric welly-driers; genuinely waterproof
clothing and dog-bags; *foie gras*, smoked salmon and potted
shrimps by instant mail order. (Where would we be without
Baxter's of Morecambe?) John Buchan and Sapper would
declare that The Breed has been hopelessly softened by all
this mollycoddling. What sort of fisherman does not even
have to bother to hang his lines out to dry at night?
Where have matters got to when some of us recoil from
getting into a draughty old soft-top Land Rover between
drives, because we are so cosy in our fan-heated Discoveries?
(Don't even think about those awful lorries or trailers into
which some shoots herd their unhappy guns.)

Guests are absurdly stroked these days. I cherish the
experience of one house, where the hostess makes it her
life's work to anticipate her friends' every overnight need.
In an idle moment during a stay there last December, I
went around my room, making a list of the goodies on
offer, which are duplicated in every other bedroom. Here it
is: Eau de cologne, Beechams Powders, Disprin, Savlon,
Bisodol, Carmen rollers, hairdryer, still and fizzy water,
Kleenex, alarm clock, sweet jar, radio, nail file, clothes

brush, fly swatter, Optrex eye lotion, toothpicks, antiseptic wipes, Deep Heat rub, Listerine, matches, torch, writing paper and envelopes, Tampax, Dettol, hairspray, nail varnish remover, hairbrush, comb, cold cream, skin lotion, hairband, books, electric fire, Panadol, Day Nurse, Floris dusting powder, shampoo, conditioner, pencil and pad, Alka-Seltzer, Night Nurse, throat lozenges, bath essence, scissors, safety pins, needle and thread, hand lotion, tweezers, Elastoplast, Dabitoff, Vaseline, toothbrushes, toothpaste, razors and shaving foam, mustard bath, bath cap, bathrobe, flannel and nail brush.

I scored a modest point by complaining that I couldn't find a shoehorn; one guest moaned about the lack of condoms, but the chatelaine retorted tartly that he was well past the age at which he could do anything with them. There are many advantages to being a guest in a grown-up household, even if you don't get taken clubbing in the village on Saturday night. The menus in that same house would make Henry VIII salivate. Aunt Dahlia's Anatole was a bungling amateur compared with the chef.

Some of you may think that all this is a mite over the top. Agreed, we want to keep a touch of rural heartiness. 'Normal temperature' in a country house in winter should require a sweater everywhere, except the sitting room in the evening and the kitchen all the time. The greatest luxury for most guests is to be told that they need not dress up for dinner. In my case, as one of life's natural scarecrows, happiest rural hours are spent in dirty jeans, with a pair of old gardening gloves sticking out of my pocket.

A picnic remains a landmark comfort test of any country household. I remember a happy day's fishing in Hampshire a year or two ago which was ruined when the lunch basket was opened. Rations were exposed to view roughly appropriate for the garrison of Kut in the later stages of the siege, when they were eating rats and the drink had run out. I wouldn't have fancied being present in my host's kitchen that night, when he launched a post-match debriefing with the catering manager. I shared his grief. A proper sporting picnic is a moment for excess. Ratty had it about right the day he took Mole sculling. Whether grouse are plentiful or otherwise, I am always grateful to be invited to an Angus moor where the luncheon menu is dominated by cold lobster, and not just *a* cold lobster, but cold lobsters sufficient to satisfy the five thousand without any time wasted on loaves and fishes.

Oh yes, there is also that most obvious of all modern indulgences – being able to decide suddenly that one feels like having a grouse for dinner in January and lifting one from the deep freeze. You will never hear me sob for the good old days when men were men and central heating was for wimps. In all respects, save traffic and new housing developments, our rural grandparents would be green with envy of the padded comfort which most of us enjoy in the English countryside today, whether we live in cottages or stately homes.

I also love Scottish sporting lodges: big ones, small ones and slightly exotic ones. The atmosphere, the decor and, above all, the sense of continuity and history are irresistible. It is delightful to be doing the same things in the same places as generations of sportsmen dead and gone: hanging grouse on the same rusty hooks in the game larder; eating dinner at the same tables; laying salmon on the same slabs (or not, as the case may be). Women sometimes protest that Highland lodge life is too male-dominated; that it is tiresome to find one's husband or loved one too worn out after pursuing wildlife all day to be capable of coherent conversation by nightfall. But I am uneasy in establishments which demand one's dinner-jacketed presence in the

drawing room on the nail at 8 p.m., at the expense of
fishing until the light is gone; then there are houses where
hostesses don't like anybody to take a rod out until there
has been a leisurely, formal deployment of guests about
tennish, after breakfast at 9 a.m. Nine a.m. indeed, in
Scotland! Half the day is gone. Those Scottish August
and September hours are too precious to waste. What real
sportsman can resist a cast or two at dawn, if conditions
are right? I appreciate that keepers, ghillies and stalkers
should be left to their just repose until a civilized hour.
But guests: why, any serious Highland guest hopes to have
a salmon, a stag or a basket of trout back from the hill by
8 a.m. Well, doesn't he?

I know one Highland lodge, redecorated from Mayfair
at astronomical cost a few years ago, where no dogs are
allowed inside. This is not a place for sportsmen. It is
merely a London boudoir that has got lost.

Real lodges have huge, century-old baths, situated in
bathrooms the size of chapels, with elaborate Victorian
patent devices for closing the plug holes. They have rendered façades, pitch-pine gunrooms, granite-chipping drives
with acres of rhododendrons shielding them from the road.
They smell of wet clothes steaming in the drying room and
dead objects lying in the hall.

Most lodge owners have a feud or two in progress with
neighbours. They speak of their rivals' sporting habits
between clenched teeth, but invite them up for an icy token
drink one evening a year, in the spirit of the Compiègne
railway carriage *circa* November 1918. It always seems a
pleasant Highland whim that the inhabitants of lodges are
referred to by neighbours as collectives. Thus, it is never:
'I wonder how the Cunningham-Bruces did on the river
today?' But rather: 'I wonder how Syre (or Clebrig or
Altnaharra) made out?' Likewise: 'We've asked Achentoul

to dinner tomorrow night,' 'It sounds as if Kildonan is having a good day on the hill,' and so on. In this way, each group of visiting or tenant Piccadilly Highlanders acquires an honorary local identity through association with the house in which they stay.

Some people kid themselves that lodge guests' exertions on the hill rule out the sort of energetical horizontal activity so popular among off-duty Shires fox-hunters. Nonsense. Plenty of torrid romances unfold in lodges. A cavalry colonel of my acquaintance is normally a model of restraint and decorum. We enjoyed watching the bonds snap one night when a drunken peer made a determined assault on the colonel's wife in the lodge drawing room after dinner, and this was pretty mild stuff by Highland standards.

Benevolent despotism is essential to lodge life. Guests may think they want to be left to make their own decisions about what they do and when. In reality, a *laissez-faire* policy is fatal. It leads to such disgraces as dressing-gowns at breakfast; failure to fish some pools or shoot the most tempting tracts of hill; last-resort afternoon trips to local tweed shops. Guests who come to Highland lodges have no business to be there at all unless they are prepared to walk, talk and at least applaud admiringly while others kill things, if they won't or can't do their share of killing for themselves. Nothing is more tiresome than to find half a house party decently exhausted by 10 p.m., while the other half has been asleep all afternoon and now yearns for a night at the bridge table.

Lodge staff rely upon those short summer months to store up anecdotage to see them through the long Highland winter. They are seldom disappointed. The keepers, ghillies and stalkers can expect a rich store of observed incompetence on the river or the hill. The stalkers on a big western Highland estate we rented some years ago spent every day on the hill for a fortnight regaling us with lurid tales about the hopelessness of their earlier guests. We quailed to imagine what they would say about us, until we achieved a notable victory by sending a rifle to the hill who walked the stalkers into pleas for longer rests and a steadier pace. The head stalker finally enquired grudgingly how old the guest was, to be suitably chastened when he learnt that he himself had the advantage of a couple of years. But then it slipped out that our guest was also Commanding Officer of 22 SAS. This was regarded by the home team as running a ringer or anyway cheating.

Lodges seldom possess meaningful gardens. A few shrubs, some wind-blown roses and a large expanse of rough-mown grass is about the limit of cultivation. The original designers, one imagines, feared that herbaceous borders and leafy bowers might distract visitors' minds from their proper business of killing things. Instead, architects expended their creative talents upon a wondrous array of outbuildings, dog kennels, game larders, pony stables and suchlike. Some of those kennels with wrought-iron railings look inviting enough to put the children in (and probably warmer than the attic bedrooms). It is a joy to see stalking ponies in the paddocks, though these days unromantic stalkers prefer their Argocats.

Notice the visitors' book on the hall table, which will invariably contain a host of tributes so fulsome and flattering that the Savoy would blush to use such guests' language to promote a hotel. These testimonials represent a catalogue of passionately and barely coded beseechings: 'Please, please, ask us again.' The best of Scottish sport cannot be rented, even by rich men; one gets there only if one is lucky enough to be invited to a lodge as a guest, by its owner. Thus does every Highland visitor suffer an agonizing week or two of suspense in January or February, before discovering whether the annual invitation is forthcoming. Oh, the shame, the misery of being crossed off. There are tales full of the black horror of Saki's short stories, about what men have done to wives whose behaviour got them blue-pencilled by Glen Slaughter, or the measure of hemlock demanded at breakfast by the rod who found himself barred from his annual week on the Spey, because he had been barmy enough to tell the ghillie what he really thought of him the previous September.

There is a macchiavellian London art dealer, mad keen on promoting his own claims to upmarket hospitality, who is said to overtip every keeper wildly, so that when next year's guest list is being discussed the tweeded minion will say dutifully to the laird, 'I'm sure we'd all like to see that nice Mr Rembrandt here again, sir.' This tactic appears to work. Never underrate the power of both the goodwill and the blackballs of all those ghillies and stalkers. Next time one of them makes indecent advances to your wife, think very carefully indeed about your priorities before encouraging her to resist.

10

My Whippet and I

I OFTEN WONDER whether it is just me, or a universal condition among dog owners, that every animal I possess clones its predecessor. That is to say, the Hastings beasts start out differently, having come from litters hundreds of miles and bloodlines apart. By the time they are, say, two or three years old each takes on the attributes of the one that went before. I have owned three black labradors over the past twenty-five years. Despite conventional-looking parentage, they have all grown up lean, rangy and – frankly – a trifle inelegant. Nicholas Soames enquires, 'How's that whippet of yours, Hastings? Still doing a bit of coursing?'

irrespective of which of my animals he is commenting upon.

One is expected to laugh heartily at this sally, but it requires superhuman restraint not to compare my dog's physique favourably with that of the former Armed Forces Minister. Whatever the shortcomings of the dog any of us possesses, it is *our* dog. We love, cherish and defend it in public places. Paddy, the current Hastings lab, matches his predecessors Stokeley and Tweedie as a tremendous enthusiast and possessor of a fine nose. On driven days, I am proud to say, he sits steady as a rock beside my peg. I claim that he would do this even if he was not anchored to a sturdy steel corkscrew and a length of rope.

My credibility suffers, however, on the sort of day I had in Norfolk a year or two ago. My host likes to arrange complex manoeuvres, which involve the guns changing position through the drives. Dogs have to expect to do likewise, and thus cannot be corkscrewed. Paddy's understanding of the rules of the game is that if he is not tethered, any pheasant which falls is fair game. An optimist, he starts running as a bird passes over my head, in order to be standing poised with jaws gaping as it descends upon him. This technique can be useful if a runner is drifting down, but of course doubles the embarrassment if I miss. Both dog and owner are exposed to ridicule. There is usually plenty of it. That day in Norfolk it was my misfortune not only to shoot worse than I have ever shot in my life, a difficult feat, but to be standing between two of the best shots in England while I did so. The drive started with the passage over my head of two fast-flying but perfectly hittable pheasants. Nothing was going on elsewhere, to distract my neighbours from watching me unleash both barrels. As the dog belted away after those remarkably healthy pheasants, their faces were a study in controlled glee. They were

too courteous to say what they thought of my marksmanship, but they let themselves go on the subject of Paddy.

'Never knew there were wild beasts loose in East Anglia
until I heard you snarling at your dog,' remarked the left-
hand gun amiably. My credibility dropped another notch
or two, as Paddy made a dash towards a bird efficiently
felled by my neighbour, before I recalled the brute to duty.
I told the rude man crossly that I had noticed him having
to do a bit of snarling on his own account, when one of his
glossy team of golden labradors started slinking towards a
pheasant in mid-drive. Those goldens were infinitely more
placid than Paddy. Like many highly bred dogs, they gave
the impression that, at their leisurely chosen pace, a dead
pheasant could develop rigor mortis before one of them
picked it up. They embodied the Etonian theory of life,
that gentlemen should not be *seen* to *try*.

Paddy goes for his bird like a rocket. Few sights give
me more pleasure than to see him course a runner. I was
once rash enough to declare in print that he had yet to
discover the joy of sex. A few weeks later, my teenage son
emerged from a shop clutching his favourite lurid teenage
magazine, shouting in excitement: 'Daddy! Daddy! Paddy's
in *Loaded*.' Good God, he was right. They had put our
innocent virgin dog's picture and my remarks in the sexual
advice column of their ghastly publication, which much
enhanced Paddy's prestige in my children's eyes, but caused
embarrassment everywhere else.

Worse followed. Paddy himself read the offending
passage in *Loaded* and gave a hearty laugh. Within days, he
was wreaking havoc by bonking every bitch on heat within
a two-mile radius of home. Within weeks he had caused a
demure spaniel down the road to give birth to a litter whose
colour and physiognomy unmistakably proclaimed their
paternity. Having already spent a fortune wiring the garden

to prevent rabbits getting in, a further fearsome outlay became necessary, to raise the netting to keep the dog from getting out.

But I suppose that in my heart I would rather own a dog whose natural urges are in sound condition, than the sort who behaves like one of those aristocratic goldens in Norfolk, who had been brought all the way from Yorkshire to procreate. Confronted with the ugly face of sex, that dog merely stood gazing at his intended with about as much excitement as a gay lobbyist in a harem. I understand that a coupling was only belatedly achieved, after much cajoling and massive injections of Viagra. Paddy argues that Viagra is for wimps.

Those who know me will say that I am just making personal excuses when I suggest that there are far more badly behaved dogs about the place than there are disciplined ones. I can claim to have Paddy reasonably well under control when he is a) tethered, or b) in my direct line of sight, or c) not under intolerable provocation from other dogs pinching his birds. But in the meantime, yes, if he gets the bit between his teeth and escapes out of sight on a shooting day and a hot scent, I can have a good deal of trouble getting him back. He harbours the belief that, once he knows he is in trouble for spurning the whistle, he is likely to fare better on his return if he brings a bird – any bird. The location and destruction of same bird can prove time-consuming.

But he does the business. And heaven knows, one sees any number of dogs who think they were put upon this earth merely to do the wrong thing. To his credit, Paddy never fights and is neither a sheep-chaser nor a fowl killer. His most charming and irresistible quality is his capacity for enjoying whatever life serves up to him. He bounds around Hyde Park or Sutherland with equal enthusiasm, jumps cheerfully into a freight box whenever he is invited to fly anywhere, and leaps equally cheerfully out again at the other end. Lifts and London flats don't bother him at all. He is touchingly trusting that all is for the best in this best of all possible worlds. He is that rare thing, a labrador who does not steal off the kitchen table and never raises his voice to anybody.

Like many shooting dogs, he is seen at his best on a grouse moor where there are not many birds to pick up. He hunts around the butt until, again and again, he wipes the eye of his rivals. But at a big pheasant drive, where a lot of birds come down, his image crumbles. Wildly overexcited, he commits that exasperating crime of running from bird to bird, picking-up and dropping them. This is my fault. Paddy is a classic example of a good dog marred by erratic handling. During the summer, he carries sticks and stones around, and he has never been properly discouraged. As a result, he has a mouth like a steel trap. Most of the time he is strictly forbidden to chase rabbits. But then we found ourselves with a rabbit problem in the garden and yes, of course, I kept sicking the dog on to every rabbit we spotted in the borders. We all know that nothing confuses dogs and children more than having the rules constantly changed around them. They need to be clear what they will be whacked for and what earns rewards. Pavlov would no doubt declare that Paddy is confused on this issue.

I was once rash enough to take him into the Game Fair scurry, which involves retrieving two dummies. He dashed for the one in the water, and brought it back with a speed and efficiency which made the heart glow. But he had not seen the second dummy thrown because he was looking at me, no doubt hoping for a chocolate biscuit. Sent in pursuit, he bounded around unconvincingly. At these affairs the handler is not allowed to do what I would do at a shoot, and walk forward myself to urge him in the right direction. That little red-faced interlude reminded me of the limitations of both of us.

All dog owners love our dogs partly because we gain so much pleasure from seeing them enjoy themselves. Paddy is a passionately keen swimmer, at his best mopping up a flight pond after dark. Yet despite this, in one respect his discipline is very good: if he comes fishing, he is happy to stand beside me all day without jumping into the river. The great Lord King, late of British Airways, had a bit of trouble a few years ago when one of his dogs leapt into the pool where he was playing a salmon and started to chase the fish across the stream. 'I shall shoot that dog if I lose this fish,' declared the Lord menacingly, in the voice that cowed so many erring cabin staff. The ghillie muttered to a bystander, 'I hope to God the bluidy animal knows he means it!' Fortunately for both, the salmon reached the net. When I am playing fish, Paddy watches with intense interest, vaguely feeling that he should be doing something but not sure what. When he sees a salmon on the bank, however, he makes it plain that he can't understand why I have been to so much trouble to catch such a dreary, slimy thing.

And since I have catalogued some of Paddy's vices, in justice, I should admit a few of my own. There was that day when I went on to the next drive, forgetting that Paddy was still hunting the last one. I have been known to forget that he is in the back of the car. Fortunately, I have not yet sunk to the depths some people achieve, of setting off home dogless. Somebody said to me glumly the other day, 'I'm afraid our family isn't very good with dogs. Things always seem to happen to them.' He described how his father had recently found his dog missing and spent two days scouring the countryside before the local garage phoned. His car was being serviced, they reminded him. Yes, he said. He knew all that. But did he know that a mechanic had noticed a whining noise and found a dog in the back of the car? I can't imagine how that man looked Ponto in the face again.

Paddy has a pretty pampered life, and a benign temper in consequence. He is almost as angry as I am when pickers-up behind our peg hoover the bag during the drive, apparently supposing that the shoot is laid on for their benefit rather than ours. He gets a bit glum in February when suddenly life starts to look empty. But I tell him that happens to lots of people, and urge him to think constructively about August. After eight years together, we can already look back on a lot of shared experiences. They can boo and jeer in Norfolk as much as they like – I will settle for Paddy's bourgeois honesty any day, rather than one of those overbred beauty queens who think they are doing a shoot a favour by turning out at all. Paddy may not have class, but I love his style.

11

RINGS OF SPARKLING WATER

SITTING IN A Tweed boat casting a forlorn fly across a hopelessly flooded stream last October, I was thinking about the character of rivers. There could scarcely be a greater contrast between the view above me of the sunlit rooftops of Coldstream, with all the appurtenances of civilization so close at hand, and the melancholy loveliness of the northern straths where I do most of my fishing. It is not that the north is in any sense better than the Borders, but merely that every river possesses an atmosphere of its own which those who seek salmon learn intimately. There are some good rivers – good in the sense that they yield plenty of fish – which somehow lack appeal, while less productive streams nonetheless possess a charm which lures back their lovers again and again. It can be the same with women, so I am told by those who know more about them than I do.

I received a charming letter the other day from a man who told me that he has fished the Ewe for twenty seasons. In recent times, he said, he has seldom taken a fish out of it. But such is his affection for well-loved pools, of which he knows every eddy, that he is still drawn there, year after year. By contrast, some of my friends pay homage to the Thurso. Yet on my only visit a few years ago – and maybe because I did not catch a fish – I found I could not warm to the flat, featureless Caithness skyline. I have never been back, which is my loss. But I did not feel I wanted to return.

One of my favourite rivers lies in the north-west of Sutherland. Almost twenty-five years ago, one Sunday on the way to other places, I drove down its length and mar-velled at the beauty and intimacy of the stream. Nowhere does it call for a long cast. It winds for six miles through narrow gorges and fern-fringed little pools, disappearing from sight of the road for a mile or so behind steep crags accessible only on foot. That Sunday in 1971 I asked who owned it. I lacked even a nodding acquaintance with the landowner, and the chance of ever getting to fish there seemed impossibly remote. But I yearned and did not forget. Twenty years later I received an unexpected invitation. I visited that river for five seasons and never got over the euphoric thrill of plying a rod on a stretch which seemed hopelessly inaccessible to me when I was twenty-five. Do not despair of anything – you never can tell.

In high, dry summer, without a spate that river is unfishable. But when there is water, oh, when there is water, it is fabulous. Five years ago I hooked a twenty-pounder in a deep ravine, which my eleven-year-old son played and landed. There have been early mornings, two hours before breakfast, standing alone on the bank in that vast northern emptiness, fighting a good fish screaming away across a big flat, when I have garnered memories I shall cherish for life.

Further east, if one had to catch a salmon to save a life, many of us would choose the Helmsdale to achieve this, because that river remains prolific in the most unpromising conditions. The dam on the loch at its head provides a lifeline for fishermen through the summer, like the hydro on the Conon. Even when nobody is doing any good on the great majority of Scottish rivers, the Helmsdale beats continue to yield ten or fifteen fish apiece, week in and week out. I sometimes think regular Helmsdale fishers, like their ghillies, grow a little blasé about what they expect from their day's sport. Those of us who get there occasionally, after being frustrated on other rivers, murmur a thanksgiving every time we put a fly on the water, because we know how lucky we are to be casting into a river which gives us a terrific chance.

The Naver, a few miles over the hill, lacks a dam and is thus much less productive in low water. Until the 1980s, for many years the river's catches almost matched those of the Helmsdale. But over the past ten or fifteen years the disparity between the sister streams has sadly widened. Year after year of low rainfall has hurt the Naver badly, and frustrated fishers of whom I have often been one. Even the wet summer of 1998 did not begin to retrieve the record until July.

Yet I retain my love for the water and the setting. Each of the Naver's six beats offers a dramatic change of mood and scenery as one rotates downriver day by day through the fishing week. The banks on the upper stretches lie open to the heather, though sheltered by some loathsome conifers beyond the road. On the middle beats sheep graze the meadows (admittedly sometimes amid an unlovely miscellany of crofters' rubbish), and great trees overhang the woody pools, so that one might be fishing a different river. In the lower reaches the landscape opens once more on to big stretches often teeming with fish. Beat six is the favourite of most regular fishers, though each, save perhaps beat three, possesses its devoted advocates. It would be foolish to deny what a sorry spectacle the river can present on a hot summer's day, when only a trickle of water slips among the mass of exposed boulders between the arid banks. But see the Naver in full flow and its magic and variety are irresistible. It is a far prettier water than the Helmsdale, where the long, winding flats can seem dispiriting, even when they are yielding fish. The Naver's remoteness – the sense of being at the furthest end of Britain – together with the view down the strath in a crystal-sharp morning light, provide golden compensation even when the salmon are uncooperative.

I have cast over quite a few western spate rivers, with varying success. Like most people, I have experienced occasional bonanzas, interspersed by long hours flicking a fly across a few yards of fishable water in a torrid heatwave. Almost without exception, those little rivers are pretty places to be, but it is useful to have a second string, a chance at a grouse or a stag, rather than to rely entirely on thunderstorms for one's sport.

After the northern streams, the mighty torrents further south make one feel like a voyager in another country. A fisher on the rivers of Sutherland glimpses only the occasional car, shepherd or tractor driver. The loudest sound might be the distant report of a rifle on the hill. Yet on Spey or Tay or Tweed there are walkers, trucks, canoeists, golfers and sometimes fellow-fishers competing from another boat or from the far bank. The prizes for which one is casting are often bigger, and there are different charms – what can match the golden colours of the trees of the Borders in autumn? But to anyone familiar with the spartan stillness of Sutherland, Tweed fishing huts, with electricity, telephone, heaters and even the odd bathroom, almost embarrass us by their opulence.

Tweed's bridges, in their pink stone, provide a peerless backdrop for some of the beats. The wildlife is richer than in the north, especially the variety of duck. Most Tweed fishers dress up much more than we northern ruffians. At the Ednam House in Kelso last autumn, I blushed at my dirty old jeans, amid all those splendidly attired figures in correct plus fours and even ties. Ties? In Sutherland we are not quite sure what a tie is. I hope the fish are suitably impressed.

In all respects, Tweed fishing is a more elegant activity than hunting the crannies of a little spate river. I have never been lucky enough to see a good Border beat when it is fishing really well, though I have caught salmon there. But I revere Tweed's grandeur, and I shall keep going back whenever anyone asks me, until one day I chance upon the river at its marvellous best. In our parents' day, of course, Tweed, Tay, Dee and Spey commanded far more respect than their smaller northern brethren because they yielded big numbers as well as big fish. Today the Tay is good at certain short seasons. Tweed flourishes chiefly in the autumn, though there are some signs of revival in the spring. The Dee – which my father mentioned with bated breath and always with the addition of the word Aberdeenshire, because in his day the Welsh Dee was also still a major force – remains much loved by its devotees, but disappointing for most of those who want to catch fish.

The Spey can produce marvellous sport, and I am very

jealous of those who can boast access to one of its great
stretches in June or July. I have only fished a couple of Spey
beats, and I would love to know the river better. Most
salmon fishers speak in hushed tones about reported triumphs from Arndilly or Tulchan. In my own experience,
after the luxury of casting over rotating beats on northern
rivers, it can become a little dreary flogging the same Spey
pools day after day. On one occasion, when I was fruitlessly
fishing a long stretch for the first time and finally got to
the bottom, I asked the ghillie what happened next. He
said, 'You go back up and start again at the top.' This is
not my idea of fun. But again, my scepticism may stem
from having missed the best beats in good conditions.

Unless one can devise some means of making a living
out of being a professional salmon fisher, about which those
who watch me cast are not sanguine, there are only just so
many rivers any of us can hope to visit during the year
while turning up at our offices often enough to earn a crust,
whether lucky enough to be invited – or even invited to
write a cheque.

It is hard to find holiday time for a new experience if,
like my correspondent from the Ewe, instinct draws us back
season after season to familiar places and pools where we
cherish memories of past victories and tragedies. Fishers are
a loyal lot, faithful to places where we have been happy in
the past, remembering almost every pull from former
seasons as we cast down a pool anew. Although I have not
fished the Borgie for years, I retain an affection for that
little Sutherland river because I cast my first futile fly for
salmon in its rocky reaches. It possesses a beauty and intimacy few streams can outdo. And I hope to keep fishing
the Naver and Helmsdale until I drop.

I have never gone to Russia to fish, not because I do
not want to, but because I so much love fishing in Scotland.

I would rather catch a few fish north of the border than wade to my waist in salmon on the Kola peninsula. Emotionally, Russia means nothing to me, while Scotland means everything. If, in addition to the pleasure of basking in the glen country, one is also lucky enough to catch fish, that is a bonus. Granted, the dilemma is growing more difficult each year, now that on many Scottish rivers one can expect to catch not merely few fish, but quite likely none at all. A host of fishermen who once migrated eagerly to Scotland each season these days go instead to Russia, Iceland, Chile, Argentina. The world has become a smaller place, its remoter pleasures much easier of access, while Scottish sport has declined. In some places, such as parts of the Hebrides, English anglers are made to feel frankly unwelcome, and poaching and sabotage are endemic. Many Scottish fishery owners, desperate to meet their fixed costs, are still asking tenants for as much money to catch nothing as once they did for the prospect of a salmon feast. Their rents are often little less than the cost of a week in Alaska or the Kola.

But for some of us, however saddened by the trends in Scottish politics as well as salmon catches, as long as north Britain offers fishermen a glimmer of hope, we shall always be there, to cherish any chance we are given in that most perfect of all sporting settings.

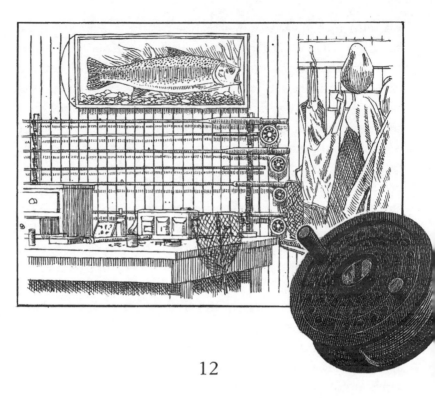

12

GROWN-UPS' TOYSHOPS

'THE PLEASURES OF fishing are chiefly to be had in rivers, lakes and tackle shops,' wrote Arthur Ransome seventy years ago, 'and of these the last are least affected by the weather.' Many men tease many women about the amount of time, money and energy they expend in fashion houses and department stores. But how many sportsmen can deny the lure of sporting gadgetry, of those fatally expensive hours lavished upon gun and tackle shops? When the mood is upon me, I rise to Farlow's window like a trout to a mayfly. I gloat upon the mail-order catalogue of Norris of Penrith. Part of the charm of any autumn visit to the Borders is the opportunity to call upon Tweedside Tackle in Kelso.

Rational sportsmen concede that the odds are slight that one will enhance one's catch by even a single salmon through fishing with a gold-plated fifteen-foot Sage, as against a workmanlike old Bruce & Walker. Who can claim to kill more pheasants with cartridges bearing the name of Holland or Purdey, than with any cut-price squib bought by the thousand from a local dealer? But many of us are not rational. Whenever we fool ourselves that we can afford it, we want the best. We can seldom resist the pleasure of using the finest equipment the market provides.

I am only an occasional stalker. A few seasons ago, I was out with a friend who had been given by his family for his fiftieth birthday a superb .243, fitted with a bipod and Austrian 6 × 42 'scope. As soon as I saw that bipod and the rock-steady shooting position it provided, I knew I had to have one. Reason tells me that, since I shoot only two or three stags a year, I have no real need to own a stalking rifle, when it is so much less bother (not least with the local constabulary) to borrow one. But today, of course, my rifle is equipped with that bipod and that Swerovski 'scope. Yes, I know that my supply of excuses for missing red deer is thus sadly diminished. But that's not the point, is it? Well, is it?

Paradoxically, however much new kit we buy, we cling to old favourites. Last summer, I stopped to buy a few flies in a little shop in Inverness-shire. Standing at the counter, I glanced down at my revolting old Barbour waistcoat, stained and torn in twenty places. This seemed a good moment to replace it, and money changed hands. Yet today, when I glance at the pegs in the back passage before I go outside, my hand strays to the dirty old coat I have worn for fifteen years because it is familiar and thus loved. The new one seldom gets an outing. On fishing days, few rods turn up on the river-bank looking scruffier than I am, partly because I am so confident of falling in. But I doubt if many fishermen have a larger collection of pristine rural garments lying idle in the cupboard at home. I keep a decent tweed suit for driven-shooting days, and was cross to be caught wearing it one afternoon when I was unexpectedly invited to abandon a flagging grouse shoot and sent stalking after lunch. That suit was fresh from the dry cleaners. The stalker was not impressed by my reluctance to descend into the sodden peat hags. Finally, inevitably, I abandoned my feeble southern scruples and wallowed in the mire behind him. But in my mean-spirited way, I yearned for filthy, old, off-the-peg breeches, the fate of which never bothers me.

Some years ago, I was given a pair of shooting stockings, of which the turnovers were tastefully embroidered with the words HOT SHOT. I possess enough sense of self-preservation not to use these for covert shooting. But my host in Sutherland was tactless enough to notice that I had worn them for an afternoon on which I missed one of his stags. They didn't contribute much to fallen dignity. I suppose we should be thankful that the boasting a few years ago about our friends' underwriting cheques is long gone, to be replaced by the wearing of stockings which proclaim BUGGER LLOYDS.

For all the pleasure of wearing well-worn old favourites, we know that the quality of sporting clothes has improved hugely in recent times. For all the affection people lavish on old brogues, there seems nothing to beat modern Timberland boots and their rivals for comfort and durability on the hill. The alleged waterproofs our parents wore were hopelessly inadequate by comparison with Gore-Tex, although it is striking that every Highland keeper sticks firmly to his tweeds, swearing that they keep him warmer even in a torrential downpour. On a dry winter's day, I still wear my Barbours with affection, and Barbour have generously repaired them again and again. But in the rain, I settle for a Schoffel jacket, or a Musto with that splendid high collar, which can do so much to keep the elements at bay. I find even a loosely cut tweed jacket clumsy when mounting a shotgun. Yet, shooting among a team of strange guns, it remains striking how often the man in the old tweeds often proves the one doing most serious damage to the birds. Real men may not eat quiche, but maybe they stick to tweeds while we wimps dally with Gore-Tex.

Caps command much affection and loyalty. We cherish the battered, shrunken, shapeless object that once hailed from Bond Street but now resembles a small haggis. A friend of mine went as a nervous adolescent to shoot with the last Duke of Marlborough. The young man's morale never recovered from the tongue-lashing he received outside the portals of Blenheim. 'Hat! Hat! There is a man here who proposes to go shooting without a hat. Get a hat, or no pheasants for you!' declared the Duke witheringly. I once turned up at a shoot to discover that I had forgotten my wellingtons. Given the enormity of my feet, there is never a hope of borrowing. You don't know the meaning of suffering until you have squelched through a wet January day in suede loafers.

Partly because we are all so wedded to old kit, sporting shops more than other establishments need to present their lures with delicacy. We want to be recognized, flattered and taken notice of. Farlow's are great at this. Brian always seems to have a moment to chat about water conditions on Tweed, or talk about the merits of new reels. Nothing is too much trouble. As a result, Farlow's have a lot of devotedly loyal customers. There is another West End tackle shop, which I had better not name. I can't imagine how it does any business at all. Browsers are received without interest or curiosity. The atmosphere is urban and impersonal, lacking any flavour of the river. The assistants are hanging about waiting for a Japanese or an American sucker with a fat cheque book. They cannot pretend to rouse any enthusiasm for some tall bloke who just wants half a dozen Grey Wulffs.

By contrast, Tweedside Tackle in Kelso offers one of the most tempting collections of sporting kit I know anywhere, and an unerring understanding of how to hook a fish. The staff will lend you any rod you want to try. How many of us, having tried one, can bear to part with it? There is also scope for a little price negotiation. In the end, no doubt, one writes pretty much the same cheque as anywhere else, but the sense of triumph about paying even a few pounds less than the price on the tag gives customers a warm glow, especially on days when there is little action on the riverbank.

I do not know how Carters Countrywear in the market place at Helmsley fares the rest of the year, but from November to February I would love to have shares in it. Some of the richest shots in the country descend on the town to demolish those high Yorkshire pheasants, and I have sometimes felt more respectful of the guns' performance at Carters' counter after the last drive, than of anything they have done in the line. Stuffed with good things, it remains one of my favourite browsing places.

There was a time when I used to be a keen shopper at the Game Fair, but experience has made me wary. For impulsive souls, the Game Fair is fatal. It encourages excess in an atmosphere in which, amid the milling throng, I cannot think sensibly. How many of us have left the Game Fair with a loaded boot and repented at leisure in the gun cupboard at home?

Even many country dwellers lament the passing of the time when all the great gunmakers were quartered in the West End, and a man who wanted a pair of 12-bores expected to fit them in Bond Street or Jermyn Street. Yes, you can today buy a gun at Asprey's. Purdey, Holland & Holland and William Evans are still within easy walk of each other. But these are only distinguished survivors of what was once a great colony of such establishments, in the days when every gentleman expected to find his gunmaker within shot of his tailor and hatter.

My father cherished his visits to Churchill's shop in Orange Street off the Haymarket, where the great gunmaker would test fire pistols in the cellar during the criminal cases in which he appeared as an expert witness. Father loved to come up from a morning as a guest in the cellar and walk to his club, still savouring the scent of powder, which in his nostrils matched the charm of any woman's perfume.

There is still a healthy tradition of sporting shops in country towns, which serve as focus of local sporting gossip, a keepers' rendezvous and general post exchange. The Rod Box in Winchester plays an important part in the lives of many chalk-stream fishers, and likewise Orvis has its shop in Stockbridge as well as Sackville Street. I have always found Orvis uncommonly friendly and helpful, though my bank manager shows signs of nervousness when he hears that I have been shopping there. Like Norris's, the Orvis catalogue is a source of unfailing delight, not least because one discovers gadgets which only the wildest imagination could conceive a practical use for.

Nowhere in Britain, I am happy to say, does the hair-raising variety of country equipment on offer match that to be found in American and European catalogues. Most of the former suggest that sportsmen are members of some fearsome paramilitary sect, unable to risk going shooting unless equipped as battlefield snipers. One of the biggest French field sports suppliers, Kettners, sell a wide range of small arms, bayonets, entrenching tools and so on, not to mention a very expensive clothing range that would get one thrown out of most self-respecting English shoots. I am wary of sportsmen in this country being encouraged to dress in full camouflage gear. Whatever its practical merits for pigeon shooting or roe stalking, it makes the wearers look disturbingly militaristic, at a time when the British public is already suspicious of field sports. Sensible muted English colours have done the job for years. They blend with the English countryside. Camouflage gear grates. I don't think it is good for our collective image.

Most of us keep a secret wish-list of toys we are determined to buy whenever our bank managers will allow. At the top of my agenda just now is a collapsible boat seat, because my long legs become so miserably cramped when I'm loch fishing in a low boat all day – oh yes, and one of those American float tubes, which look as if they would be great fun for fishing in remote little lochs in Scotland. In the dock under oath, I could not for a millisecond argue that I *need* either of these objects. I doubt if I would use either more than twice a year. But I *want* them terribly. I suppose that is why most tackle shops tend to be so civil to gullible trout like me. For some of us, it is duffer's fortnight all year around.

13

SYNDICATE SHOOTING

SOMEBODY ASKED ME recently if I would like to join a local shooting syndicate – nice people, pretty place, modest cheque. I passed. Much as I like both the people and the place, my syndicate days are over. Every year I take a shooting day or two to repay hospitality to friends, and we all enjoy ourselves. But nowadays, I don't feel able to cope with belonging to a syndicate. The emotional (not to mention financial) tensions call for stoicism of a heroic order. A good many of us baulk that jump if we can.

When I was younger, however, like most people, I would have got no shooting at all if I had not joined a syndicate.

I was twenty-three when I first took a half-gun in a Hampshire shoot owned by a friend of my father. A rotund, amiable, prosperous farmer, Tom took his pleasures indulgently and found lunch the most agreeable of them. I was much too young to fit in comfortably with the other guns, and too hyperactive to enjoy his leisurely approach. This was usually characterized by the cancellation of the last drive. 'They'll all be there for another day,' he would say, pottering cheerfully off homewards towards the decanter. But I drove away sulking about how much more that day had cost me than I could afford. My half-gun would not be there next time. On one coveted occasion when I was due to shoot, I found myself stuck in a blizzard in Northern Ireland on a newspaper assignment. By Herculean efforts I got back to London, and slithered through the snowdrifts to the estate, arriving exhausted but triumphant at 9.15 a.m. on Saturday morning.

My host appeared bewildered at his front door. 'Shoot? What shoot? I didn't bother to ring you, because I didn't think anyone but a madman would imagine that we could go out in these conditions.' I retired crestfallen to Belfast, and soon afterwards resigned from the syndicate, unlamented. I was too callow, and the mood of the shoot too elderly, for us to suit each other. The bills were ruinous – about a sixth of my net income at the time.

A year or two later, no richer and no wiser, I took another half-gun in another South of England shoot. I quickly learnt that the team was rent by dissension. Some guns were morbidly suspicious that they were deliberately excluded from the best days. Others raged about numbering. Some pegs, it was true, seemed doomed all day. The paranoiacs persuaded themselves that this was the result of deliberate persecution by our landlord. He took the view that, since the shoot was on his estate, it could be governed by his whims, of which there were plenty. In reality, as we all know, successful syndicates depend not only upon being fair to all members, but on being seen to be so. The chief reason many landowners nowadays renounce syndicates in favour of letting days is precisely because with let days, there is less scope for wrangling. You pays your money, and your team get their birds.

Soon after I was married, I exchanged my southern half-gun for another with a buccaneering shoot in Lincolnshire. This was smaller, cheaper and more equitably run. I enjoyed the days trawling hedges and ditches, taking it in turns to walk or beat. But as a Londoner, I was still an outsider among a group of Midlanders who had known each other all their lives. It is always nicest to shoot among close friends. I only achieved this ten years later, when four of us started a small syndicate on an estate in Northamptonshire, only a couple of miles away from my house. Its chief joy was the part-time keeper, a wonderful Scots tractor-driver in his sixties who threw himself heart and soul into the pheasants, aided by his daughter and periodic spells of manual labour contributed by ourselves. This was the beginning of one of the happiest periods of my shooting life. It was without pretension, it was full of laughs, and with only four of us in it we managed not to quarrel about money – or not much, anyway.

We enjoyed the fencing and wood-cutting on summer Sunday mornings under the sceptical eye of Morris, forever scornful of our manual incompetence. We walked in line behind the harrow throwing out artichokes, and chainsawed the fringes of overgrown flight ponds and coverts. At last, I savoured the sense of having a real stake in the ground we were shooting, knowing the spinneys and paying a weekly visit to Morris and the pheasants through the rearing season. There were occasional differences among the four of us about ways and means, but on the whole we were a harmonious group (they might say that it was because they showed Olympian restraint about my excesses). Four is surely the ideal number for a syndicate. When you have eight or nine guns, some tension becomes inevitable, and there tends to be a steady 'churn' of guns with all the bother of getting to know new people.

Our relations with the local hunt were never warm, because in the shires most fox-hunters share an unshakeable conviction that shooters are trespassing on their turf. The shooters, in our turn, never forget that we are paying for rights on the land, while hunts are not. I am sure remarks like this will provoke some fox-hunting readers to tell me I am talking nonsense, that most Shire hunts rub along very well with shoots. But I have eavesdropped at enough well-lubricated Shires dinner parties to know how both sides really feel. 'I'll get that stupid bugger Hastings out of that silly little shoot of his if it's the last thing I do,' to quote a celebrated local Master on a Saturday night a decade ago. He believed the fact that a shoot had been created on traditional hunting turf was insult enough. A week after that remark was repeated to me, I shot a fox, coolly, secretly and pleasurably. Even a Northumbrian fox-hunting friend of mine was shocked when he came down our way as a guest and held open a gate for a hundred-odd hunt followers. He remarked that only three of them made any gesture of acknowledgement. That's the sort of thing which has helped to make fox-hunters an endangered species, and has created the current problems in Leicestershire where some estates are declining to give fox-hunters access until shooting is over.

Despite the less appealing sort of fox-hunter, we had ten wonderfully happy years from that Northamptonshire syndicate, with a lot of laughter and sport, even if some of those pheasants had taken flying lessons from the RAF's contour-chasers. It was the birds' misfortune to be up against guns who took the view that if pheasants flew in an unsporting fashion, they must expect retaliation with equal lack of scruple.

At the risk of upsetting more high-minded sportsmen, I would say the chief reason our syndicate was a success, jolly company apart, was that it did not cost much. All of us knew we were getting our days and our pheasants pretty cheaply. Rancour sets in where guns are paying hideously large sums of money, and thus expect correspondingly extravagant results. Even the most saintly syndicate member feels a bit miffed if he has paid a lot of money and hardly gets a shot all day. We are supposed to tell each other that this is not what sport is about, that we should accept the luck of the game. But at heart, most syndicate shooters are as cost-conscious as anybody else. That has always been one of the merits of rough-shooting in Ireland: since it costs next to nothing, nobody cares too much about what does, or does not, happen.

Unless one is a natural megalomaniac, running a syndicate is a thankless task. There are some places where the man who does the job expects to be rewarded by getting his own shooting for nothing. Most of us would not sign up to that sort of deal, any more than we would take a day on an estate where the landlord keeps a gun for himself while the tenant pays the bill. A decent syndicate is a democracy, where decisions are discussed and agreed in advance, and whoever is in charge pays the same stake as everybody else. Nobody has any business to run a shoot unless he can forecast costs with reasonable accuracy, and stick within, say, £500 of an agreed budget.

Maybe I have been unlucky in seeing too many ropy syndicates in action. There are plenty which are impeccably run, and in which some members happily persevere season after season. But familiarity and friendship are so precious to the success of most shooting days that it is hard not to lose something when these things are in short supply or missing altogether.

14

FLY FEVER

WHEN THAT GREAT Sutherland fisher Willie Gunn died, although I never met him, I doffed my cap in spirit. For a good while now, I have seldom fished for salmon with any other fly than that which bears his name. Long ago, I became a devotee of the school which holds that, in catching salmon, changing fly patterns counts for little. The state of the river and the mood of the fish are the most important elements. Then comes luck and after that commitment. Then follow the presentation of the fly and – a long way behind – its size. In my more rational moments, I do not think it matters a fig to a fish whether he is confronted

with a Hairy Mary, a Garry Dog or a Willie Gunn. I fish a
lot with Willie Gunns because I like the look of them, and
they have often worked for me. I would never venture to
tell the man down the bank that he is wrong to be using
a Stoat's Tail – if it works for him.

But now I hear the odd reader who has glimpsed my
fly box(es) say, 'Yet if all that Hastings professes about his
own approach is true, why does he carry about with him
two or three hundred flies, and even cast with several dozen
of them over a week?'

Ah, sceptical reader, you missed my line above, about
rational behaviour. I think rationally about fishing when I
am sitting at home, as I am now, or when I am catching
fish. I cease to behave rationally – and I submit that many
other anglers do likewise – when I am on the river-bank
and *not* catching fish. Take the summer of 1996, amid all
those days when one was fiddling around killing time, and
certainly not salmon, in an interminable heatwave on
various Sutherland beats. The ghillies took the view that
there was scarcely a cat's chance of catching anything, and
certainly none after, say, 7 a.m. There we were, with nothing
else to do and nowhere else to go. After the first hour or
two plying the pools with a very small fly on a very fine
cast, we began to experiment. First, we tried other patterns
of the same trifling size, then we tried surprising the fish
with unexpected flies in unexpected places.

Now, I know and you know that in the unlikely event
I had been successful in persuading one of those bored, stale
fish to take a large Garry Dog, it is plausible that I would
have been equally successful had I presented the same fish
in the same manner with a small Willie Gunn. But we
shall never know because, like most fishermen in desperate
circumstances, I had resorted to desperate methods, and the

desperate method may chance to be the one that prevails. Confusing isn't it?

My essential thesis is that while rationally I know that I could have fished all week with my tiny Willie Gunn with an equal chance of success, most of us start to behave foolishly when we have fished for hours, or days, without moving a salmon. Following the argument a little further, we might agree that Farlow's and its counterparts would go out of business, but for the fact that salmon fishermen are more often casting in unfavourable conditions than favourable ones. What Scottish fisher who experienced the droughts of 1996 and 1997 would have guessed that, for most of 1998, he would be striving against the odds to catch the attention of a fish with a huge fly in an almost permanent flood? You never can tell. You can only be sure that conditions will be less than ideal most of the time.

Changing flies and enriching tackle shops are functions of failure. When we are catching fish, we seldom change fly patterns. Indeed, on one of those miraculous days when we land five, six or seven salmon, we often stick obsessively to the tattered, almost hairless, hook which has brought us success. Tackle shops do not want us to have many days like that. Rather, they yearn for desperate men who are driven to try anything to rouse a fish's interest, who will indeed often telephone their emporia from the river-bank in despair, asking to be sent *everything*.

The conceits of fly-choosers change from generation to generation. In 1840, James Wilson extolled the merits of the Grizzly King, Sam Slick, Long Tom, the Professor, the Greenmantle with as much enthusiasm as I praise the Willie Gunn 160 years later. The underlying principle remains the same. Wilson himself avowed, 'It may be stated at once, and without reservation, that so far from imitating nature, the makers of salmon flies can scarcely form these in too unnatural and extravagant a manner.'

Sydney Buxton, a splendid specimen of the Edwardian sporting politician, wrote sardonically in 1902, 'The fashion in salmon flies varies almost as much as that in ladies' bonnets or in men-of-war; for while a trout fly is tied to please the fancy of the trout, a salmon fly is composed to attract the fancy of the fisherman.'

Plus ça change. Like most fishermen, I now possess an absurdly large collection of flies. Yet still I find that, on the day and on the river, I am usually without the exact variation the situation demands. On Tweed in October I have plenty of one-inch weighted tubes, masses of three-inch weighted tubes, but no two-inch weighted tubes such as the ghillie declares indispensable. The same problem recurs on the Helmsdale in August with Waddingtons, on the Naver in May with . . . Well, you get the idea. I suppose I should try a fly none of you will have heard of, called the Conqueror. So far as I know, only one of them exists – specially tied for me as a gift from the Flyfishers' Club, among the most flattering and pleasing presents I have ever received. The trouble is that this splendid object hangs in a frame on the wall at home beside my rod rack. I have never dared use it. Put to the test in hopeless conditions on a scorching July day in Sutherland, I am convinced any salmon would be as impressed as I am by the Conqueror. Memo to myself: have another dozen tied, to cram into the fly boxes.

Yet in discussing the order of importance in determining factors for success on a salmon river, I doubt whether many experienced fishermen would dissent from that which I quoted at the outset. If a river is in good order and fish are moving well, then any damn fool can prosper and often does so. Luck plays a much greater part on a salmon river than on a trout stream. Commitment is a word I often use, which might translate as determination. This is not only a matter of how many hours one spends on the river, it is also a function of concentration and, yes, the killer instinct, the will to prevail. I can think of no other reason why some moderate fishermen like me catch quite a lot of fish: we care more passionately about success than some others who value lunch or teatime or even sex, who think it is a bit sub-standard to go on flogging the water at all hours.

I will go on covering the water at any time when there is a legal chance of taking a fish. I hate to admit defeat even in the most unpromising conditions, though it is even more galling to find that perseverance has been outdone by sheer skill. I have seldom felt crosser than at the moment of 1995 when I walked up from one of the Naver beats after two days of empty-handed casting, to meet the team from the beat above with four salmon in the back of their car. Fishing is not a competitive activity, but . . .

That particular group have a reputation not merely as committed on-the-river-at-5 a.m.-in-summer-sunshine fishers, but also as exceptional presenters of flies. I am confident of my commitment, but conscious of my limitations as a presenter, especially in poor conditions. We all recognize that a bad cast can sometimes catch a fish. I have profited from this fact more often than most. But I also know enough to be conscious when I am wasting precious time and water. For instance, casting into a wind, again and again my fly lands on the water amid a dreaded curl of nylon. In other words, it will not begin to show properly until it has drifted at least a couple of yards across the current to straighten the line. If one goes on fishing like that all day, the cumulative waste of energy and potential hooked salmon is prodigious. Now that I get to do a lot of fishing, and can no longer produce all my old excuses as a novice, I am ashamed of my own performance on the back cast. I have only a rudimentary grasp of spey casting. If I am throwing a line with trees or a steep bank behind me, the consequences for Farlow's are profitable.

Each spring I vow that this will be the one in which, at last, I learn spey casting properly. The late Hugh Falkus used to send kind messages from Cumbria, offering to teach me. I claimed that I could not spare two days for the lessons. But if I added together the hours I have wasted on salmon beats, because of the failings of my technique, then of course I should have done the only sensible thing, and made time to learn more. This goes for a lot of us.

The aspect of salmon fishing which I have omitted thus far, is that of knowing the river. Those of us who only see a given beat for a week a year cannot hope to read the current in all its moods and at all heights. Ghillies and proprietors will always have a big advantage. They can usually wipe our eyes if they put their minds to it, and so they should. A variation in height of a few inches one way or the other changes the nature of most lies on most salmon beats, and these subtleties can only be appreciated by a fisher who knows intimately what lies beneath the surface of every pool, as the casual visitor cannot.

Few of us who are not very old or very rich get the chance to become familiar with every nuance of a beat. But then again, if the river lost its mystery, if we felt confident of what lay beneath that shimmering, liquid sheen, salmon fishing would lose a vital part of its mystery and its magic.

15

VILLAGE LIFE

THERE IS A telling passage in George Eliot's *Silas Marner* where the author remarks how little theft there was in Marner's village, not because the villagers were specially honest, but because if they stole: 'how could they have spent the money without betraying themselves? They would be obliged to "run away" – a course as dark and dubious as a balloon journey.'

A lot of nonsense is talked about people today being inherently more dishonest than they used to be. In reality, what is new is the infinite scope which mobility provides for profiting from crime, and the fact that we all possess a lot more worth stealing. Silas Marner's folk had to walk. Today, almost everyone has a car, and can use it for good or ill to roam a range unimaginably wider than that of our ancestors.

Far fewer of us belong to a place, as they did – growing up, going to school, working and living in the same rural community from cradle to grave. That wonderful recent play *The Weir*, by Conor McPherson, explores the behaviour of a group of locals in a pub in the west of Ireland, confronted by a new arrival from Dublin, a young woman who shows her alien colours by asking for a glass of white wine. The four men in the play have known each other's every whim and way for decades. The girl is a 'blow-in', an outsider. Seeing *The Weir* recently, I was touched by the junction with my own experience. Most of my life I have been a 'blow-in' to a succession of rural communities, sometimes for years, without becoming truly part of any.

Across much of rural Britain today there are far more 'blow-ins' like me than there are deeply rooted local people. The Scottish Highlands are thickly populated with English 'white settlers', many of whom behave more assertively, for better or worse, than the natives. In a host of English villages, retired people moving into an area late in life become the bastions of the church, the village hall, the fête, the parish council. The first condition for becoming part of any rural community is that one should have time. Watching the pub scene in *The Weir*, in which the group at the bar spins away an evening in gossip and reminiscence, I reflected that I have never in my life spent a whole evening in a country pub. I have always gone into the local for a purpose – to get a drink, to eat, to meet a friend. Purpose served, I pay and go, usually inside the half-hour. If you belong, you don't behave like that.

I was once roundly ticked off by a local vicar for my

impatience in the village shop, where I shuffled my feet irritably as I waited for Mrs Jones to finish exchanging an interminable crosstalk with Mrs Smith behind the counter over her purchase of ten cigarettes. 'You ought to understand,' said the vicar, 'that the most important things exchanged across the counters of village shops are not goods, but human contacts.' He was right. I knew that the fact I always professed to be in a hurry was one of the defining marks of the townie, the weekender, the 'blow-in', as against the authentic local. I had no expectation of being buried in the churchyard, of seeing young village oaks grow to maturity, any more than I possessed shared memories of the village school. It is because so many of us choose to conduct swift and impersonal transactions through the supermarket checkout that the village shop is under threat.

That village was simply somewhere that I happened to be living, rather than somewhere to which I belonged. The same applied even more emphatically when we lived in rural Ireland for a couple of years, and in assorted English cottages when I was younger. Rural communities which prosper need a core of local limpets, anchored to the village rock throughout their lives, amid the shifting population which comes and goes with the tides and seasons, the chances of employment and changes of family circumstances. When money has to be raised for local causes, cheques are often forthcoming from the 'blow-ins', and very useful they are. But the greater needs of all communities, which our kind find harder to meet, are those of time and commitment.

My respect grows every year for those – often busier people than me – who make hours to cherish the church, serve on the parish council, run stalls for the fête. Without them the rural life we all profess to love would be doomed. If a principle was adopted by politicians as well as voters,

that only those willing to work their passage in the countryside were entitled to make its policies, Countryside Marches
would become unnecessary.

It would be wrong to idealize the old communities
George Eliot knew, to which every man and woman perforce
belonged. The inhabitants lacked the mobility to have any
choice. For every contented rustic, there was in each village
a share of unhappy prisoners stifled by the pettiness, the
feuds, the intolerances and jealousies of a small place that
knew little of the outside world. Jane Austen's novels
emphasize the fact that, even for the squirearchy, the choice
of marriage partners usually had to be made within a
pitifully narrow field of neighbours, within coach-visiting
distance. And harnessing the horses was not a matter to be
undertaken lightly, nor two days' running.

As late as the 1950s, in the village where I spent much
of my childhood a mere forty-five miles from London, there
were still a good many people who had never visited the
capital, and some who had seldom travelled the nine miles
to Reading. In the country today, we profit from the fact
that we can choose friends and dining companions across a
twenty-, thirty- even forty-mile radius. The children of even
the most committed 'belonger' in a village are liable to
produce husbands or wives from anywhere in Britain. They
may not be happier people than our rustic forefathers, but
they can exploit a freedom and choice which are virtues for
any society.

I regret my lack of deep roots in the countryside, a
necessary price for any of us who earn our livings from the
city. It seems time to be putting some down. When I am
able to spend less time working and travelling, I hope
I can start to work my passage towards acceptance as a
participating member of a community, rather than as
a passenger. Rural areas need people to share in their care

all the time, not merely at weekends. Many of the political problems facing the countryside today stem from the fact that the people most eager to interfere with it and change its ways are those who have never even aspired to belong.

For ten years I ran a shoot on an estate, where at the outset all the village houses were tenanted. But over that decade the village population gradually changed, as in so many similar communities up and down the country. Houses were sold off. We used to drive a belt of the trees alongside a road, with one gun walking on the verge. But in the early 1990s, we stopped doing so, in the face of some passing drivers' outrage, which extended on one occasion to telephoning the police.

At another drive, a couple of guns used to stand in the estate village. On a Saturday in our last season, I was blazing away enthusiastically when a woman came out of a farmhouse. 'I am not against shooting,' she said, 'but we are not estate tenants. We bought this house. I do not consider that, as the price of living here, we have to put up with you firing guns twenty yards from my front door and dropping pheasants into my garden.'

I retreated crestfallen, because I could not argue with her. In that village, as in a host of others, the old structure wherein residents had a close personal relationship with the estate was dying. And as the number of agricultural workers has declined, so has the acquiescence of some 'ordinary country people' in field sports. At a shoot in the north of England a year or two ago, we were talking about the problems of raising membership of the field sports organizations. One of the guns gestured towards the beaters: 'They love shooting – but will they put a penny towards any of the organizations? No. They think it's for us to do that.'

The Countryside Rally and the Countryside March yielded big turnouts from every part of the social spectrum.

But as the threat to field sports has grown, many of us have been thinking hard about the relationship between town and country, and about how better to make rural voices count. Labour politicians like to quote opinion polls, which show that a substantial share even of country dwellers want to see fox-hunting banned.

These polls reflect the social trend I touched on above: there are more and more people living in the country whose acquaintance with its ways is slight, and who earn their livings elsewhere. In particular, most 'incomers' reject any notion of deference to local landowners. They resent restrictions upon freedom to walk or play in the fields and woods beside which they live. Unless the local keeper is a man of exceptional charm and tact, he often becomes the focus of incomers' dislike and resentment of the alleged tyranny of land ownership and the supposed barbarism of rural pastimes. It was a landowner who said to me recently, 'People like us have to accept the consequences of our own actions: over the past generation or two, we've made a lot of money by selling off houses and cottages we don't need any more for estate workers to new people. But the price we pay is that we have lost control of our local environment.'

Almost all farmers would acknowledge the change in attitudes among their employees over the past twenty or thirty years: workers want their own homes rather than tied cottages, pension rights rather than free milk and suchlike. Younger men do not want an obligation to their employers, they want a level playing field between two freely contracting parties, though they would phrase it less pompously.

Now, that brings me back to field sports, and to those beaters I mentioned above who couldn't see why they should bother to join the Countryside Alliance. If they have access to shooting only through beating and a beaters' day at the end of the season, they are indeed unlikely to feel they have the same stake in the sport as somebody who shoots driven pheasants thirty days a year. Somebody wrote to me the other day, asking if I could think of anywhere, within thirty miles of Hungerford, where he could rent a bit of rough-shooting for himself and his boys. I am no fount of local wisdom, but I had to answer that I imagined almost every acre is tied up in driven shoots. 'A bit of shooting' has become incredibly hard to find in the South of England for a man unable to put his hand pretty deep in his pocket. Even pigeon decoying is getting hard to come by.

Yes, I know about the wildfowlers and the many rough-shooters towards the northern and western edges of this crowded island. But my fear is that the threat of hostile legislation against shooting will intensify if the sport is perceived, even by many genuine country people, to be a rarefied pastime for would-be toffs. The more people who can be helped to enjoy opportunities to go rough-shooting, who can be brought into the sport, the safer its future is likely to be. Governments in general, the present Labour government in particular, are hugely influenced by cold calculation of numbers in deciding which way to jump politically: 'How many divisions has the Pope?'

The glee of many Labour MPs about their alleged class-war victory in the last Commons fox-hunting vote empha-sizes the political importance of being able to demonstrate the wide, popular base of shooting, rather than allowing critics to focus on tycoons' mass slaughter in Surrey. We know that fishing's salvation lies in the size of its constitu-ency, rather than in the sort of nonsense peddled by Mr Mike Foster MP, who claims that it is less cruel.

Nothing can change the reality, that new people are moving into countryside, as the number of people who work on and understand the land declines. But the need has never been greater for the followers of country sports to encourage and assist newcomers to participate in them, however and whenever they can. Save in Britain's remote wilderness, there will be no new generation of deferential tenants and rustics – and, in many respects, a good thing too. But we cannot afford to allow the divide to deepen, between the countryside's traditional inhabitants – the 'belongers' – and the new breed of incomers.

Many of the latter are sceptical, if not hostile, towards field sports and traditional patterns of land ownership. Their reasoning may seem flawed or downright foolish, but their votes are as good as anyone else's. Unless a portion at least of the huge influx of newcomers to the countryside can be wooed to its ways, then the next generation of 'blow-ins' could have it in their power to destroy them.

16

THANKS TO THE KEEPERS

IT IS PROBABLY a delusion to imagine that the local
gamekeeper was ever a popular figure, other than with
those who profited from his services. In the eighteenth or
nineteenth centuries few villages warmed to the landlord's
nark, the setter of mantraps, whacker of poachers and exter-
minator of stray dogs and cats. To this day, if a beloved pet
goes absent without leave, Mrs Turnstile from Rose Cottage
is more likely to point the finger of blame at the wicked
keeper over on the estate, rather than at guilty Aunt Ethel,
who was in reality the one that turned moggie into a useful

Wendy-house rug by driving the Renault over it in the dark at 40mph.

It is the business of keepers to say 'thou shalt not' to almost everybody except the guns and sometimes to them as well. Nancy Mitford painted a bleakly satirical portrait of her siblings' war against Uncle Matthew's keeper, Craven, with his unspeakable instruments of cruelty and death. Trollope regarded keepers with the chronic suspicion of a fox-hunter: men who were forever doing a noble quarry to death in dark corners, unstopping earths and – heaven help us – selling bag foxes.

In times past, gamekeepers were vested with all the authority which stemmed from being private constables of landowners, who wielded immense economic, political and social power in their regions. It was a brave man who was prepared to cross a grandee's keeper. Today, by contrast, landowners are an endangered species, beset by lobbies and political adversaries, who question their right to untrammelled stewardship of their acres. The gamekeeper represents the most controversial aspect of private possession of the countryside, and his behaviour is thus under special scrutiny.

This is a confusing and difficult position for most men. On the one hand, a keeper's job remains what it always has been – to present birds to best advantage on the day, for his employer's shoot. On the other, however, the brutal realities of what he needs to do in order to provide sport are subject to mounting attention and criticism. Keepers' control of vermin and raptors is under the microscope, together with their treatment of straying dogs and cats. The traditional problems of poaching have receded now that there is only a negligible commercial market for game. Walkers with dogs present a growing difficulty, so too in some areas do gypsies bent on coursing hares, who can display extraordinary violence if they are thwarted. Magistrates are seldom notably sympathetic to game preservers these days, and relations with the police have deteriorated sadly in some areas. One day last winter, a keeper I know in Gloucestershire was infuriated to find his game cart followed into a field on the shoot by a passing patrol car, asking questions about its absence of a number plate and tail lights. The keeper said he had often helped the police over the years in identifying and picking up criminals of one sort or another. He found this piece of casual harassment a poor return. Likewise, some stalkers report growing friction with Scottish forces, looking for trouble about firearms certificates.

More and more people want to walk on the land. Especially in the South of England, their presence increases the difficulties of those seeking to preserve game. Public access to the countryside, and thus disturbance of wildlife on private land, must increase over the next generation. Unless government completely loses its head, some restrictions will persist about where the public can go and when. But the gamekeeper will be the man in the front line, dealing with the problems posed by access. Many keepers are instinctively solitary figures, who cherish a life of which much is spent alone in wild places. Yet, in the new world, they will need exceptional patience and diplomatic skill to cope with new pressures.

It is depressing for a man who has nurtured wildlife all his days to see himself portrayed in parts of the media as a professional assassin. Most television questioning of keepers is of the 'When did you last beat your wife?' persuasion – or rather 'When did you last murder a dog/hawk/cat?' If one is not paranoid on starting a gamekeeping career, there must be every excuse for becoming so after listening to modern MPs talking about the countryside.

Gamekeeping has diversified in recent years – most numerous today are the part-timers who look after a few birds for a farmer or small syndicate because they love having a personal stake in a patch of countryside and in shooting. They are all passionate enthusiasts, although their standard of competence varies wildly. The best are very good indeed. Then there is a diminishing band of lucky ones, who hold long tenure on traditional estates, working for one man for many years and producing birds every shooting day for familiar expectations and a team of invited guns. For everybody concerned the continuity is delightful, though there can be problems as a much-loved veteran ages and grows set in his ways. Finally, there are the keepers who face the most taxing task of all: showing birds on industrial principles for large estates where most of the shooting is let. Each week, sometimes each day, they deal with guns whose competence and manners vary wildly. The tips of some visitors vacillate according to the amount of forelock-tugging on offer, rather than the quality of the pheasants.

How depressing it must be for a keeper, who worries himself to distraction about getting a shooting day right, to be confronted with a team that can't shoot for nuts, or are rude to the beaters, or simply treat the whole day like a sporting visit to a McDonalds takeaway. I shot appallingly on a couple of days recently. It wasn't my host whom I felt deserved an apology, it was his keeper.

Not that all keepers are saints. Some are notoriously lazy – for instance, about taking the trouble to shift guns when a wind makes it plain that birds will not favour familiar pegs. It is pretty damn silly to stand in a contrary gale, as one sometimes does, and watch a mass of birds pouring back over the beaters because nobody has thought to move the line. I halved the tip I was expected to give the keeper at a commercial shoot in Yorkshire last season because he couldn't be bothered to stop the pickers-up pinching every bird from my dog.

At shoots where the birds fly consistently poorly – and there are plenty of them – it is hard for an outsider to tell whether this is because the lie of the land is hopeless, the keeper doesn't know what he's doing, or the owner simply likes to shoot lots of low birds. In the latter case, one wonders what goes through a keeper's mind, watching guns demolish pheasants on the ends of their barrels. Indifference? Shame? Disgust? Perhaps one gets used to anything.

The biggest single problem for the modern gamekeeper, and especially the upland keeper, is that of vermin control. Beyond the objections to many traditional methods of killing vermin, the range of protected species grows ever longer. It almost defies belief that cormorants, for example, enjoy the full protection of the law when we see so many of them and know how much havoc they wreak in fisheries. The Game Conservancy and the RSPB's recent Langholm report showed conclusively the devastating impact on a grouse moor of allowing the unchecked spread of raptors. No reasonable person wants a return to the nineteenth-century practice of exterminating hawks on shoots, not least by the awful cruelty of pole traps. In more recent times, a tacit balance has been struck, whereby every estate has its hawks and often eagles, but some restraint on numbers is discreetly maintained. Now, however, for the raptor fanatics this is not enough. Despite the unquestioned large increase in raptor numbers, the RSPB and others demand the summary prosecution of any gamekeeper or landowner found to be killing any raptor in any circumstances. They continue to resist the Game Conservancy's sensible proposals for licensed transfer of raptors from areas where there are obviously too many, to places where they can do less harm.

RSPB watchers are devoting ever more funds and energy to raptor protection, and the society shamelessly retreated from accepting the implications of the Langholm report, when this made it plain that for any grouse moor to prosper, raptor numbers must be controlled. It seems strange that an organization allegedly devoted to birds should ruthlessly promote the welfare of certain species at the expense of others, for of course raptors flourish through predation. The RSPB sees nothing perverse about arguing that while raptors must in no circumstances be killed to preserve a balance of nature, their victims may be killed at will to provide nourishment for raptors. The society seems unwilling to acknowledge the consequences for the uplands of an environment where raptors are now at the top of a food chain, in which there are no longer wolves or other greater predators to compete for mastery and thus maintain the historic balance. Michael Wigan has written, 'Unlike birdwatchers elsewhere, it appears that British birdwatchers are unprepared to take on board the concept of game-shooting as an intrinsically conservationist form of man-agement.'

Many upland gamekeepers sincerely fear for their livings, in this new world in which the protectors of raptors are kings. If keepers cannot produce game, their jobs will go. If raptors continue to proliferate, the historic conse-quences for grouse will be desperate all over this island. But no keeper's employer can protect him if he is found to be killing hawks. The consequence is an uneasy tacit understanding, fraught with peril for all those who care about the countryside and field sports, which places an unjust burden upon the keeper. It is he, and not his employer, who appears in the dock if he breaks the law. Yet some employers expect their keepers to do whatever is necessary to produce sport. They look the other way about how this is done, leaving the keeper with a responsibility that could cost him his livelihood. We are going to hear a great deal more about the vermin and raptor issue in the years ahead. It threatens gamekeeping and thus shooting. I see no comfortable answer to the dilemma, because the power of the RSPB seems likely to ensure that the public, and the body politic, are uncompromising in their attitude to protected species.

If I was a gamekeeper, I would resent intensely the practice of encouraging outrageous tipping which has become routine at some big shoots. This is merely a form of showing off. The richest and most extrovert shot I know likes to end the day by turning to fellow guns and saying, 'I think it should be a hundred pounds, don't you?' In a pig's ear. A gun's tip to the keeper should be a token of personal appreciation, not a major industrial investment. People who own big shoots may want to pay their keepers over the odds and good luck to them. A peer early this century earned much appreciation, especially from young guests, by sticking a card in their rooms: 'Kindly do not offer gratuities to the servants. Lord Derby pays his staff properly.' But all this three-figure-tipping stuff is for the sort of guns who think it is smart to shop at Harrods.

It is never encouraging to meet a noisy or wildly over-weight keeper. I know one who is always making asides in clumsy stage whispers within earshot of the guns, rolling his eyes the while: 'God save us from idle underkeepers!', 'What can you do if everybody lets you down?' or merely noisy imprecations to his line, 'Beat it on now! Beat it on out!' He is what is best described as an old soldier, who knows every dodge and line of cow manure in the business, except how to show pheasants. The keeper at one famous Devon high-pheasant shoot is a notorious shouter – during drives he bawls at guns, beaters, pickers-up and, personally,

I could never believe in him as a keeper in consequence. He also flatters guns outrageously about their performance, which has nothing to do with increasing their confidence and everything to do with upping his own tip.

The most distinguished practitioners of their art are almost all quiet, discreet men. The charm and unobtrusive effectiveness of men like Andrew Hill at Yattendon, Trevor Wilson at Kepwick or Brian Wells at Dumbleton contribute immensely to the pleasure of any shooting day. The best keepers offer advice about what to expect the birds to do, especially to a gun on a flank peg and, better still, a few hints if one is missing everything. Sympathy is what we need most from nannies and keepers. If one is a newcomer to a shoot, it is also nice to be told what is going on – where the beaters are coming from, which way should we expect the birds and so on. I always enjoy being a walking gun because one sees so much more of the ground, the beaters – and often, of the game. Any gun who does not care about what is going on beyond the hedge, out of sight, doesn't deserve to be shooting in the first place.

The keeper, in his turn, wants and almost always deserves appreciation – for his triumphs and for his difficulties. Most work 365 days a year, or pretty close to that, to produce, say, fifteen or twenty days' shooting in a season, representing the fruit of all his labours. For a gun, if a drive is wrecked by a fox running through or all the birds going back in a high wind, it is merely a little incident worth a line in the gamebook. But for the master of ceremonies, a blow of that sort knocks a hole in one of the biggest days of his year. Or at least, if he doesn't feel like that then he is the wrong kind of gamekeeper.

Those of us who are only part-time countrymen cherish huge respect for the good keepers, men whose lives are committed to the environment in which they work. They understand the land in a way most of us can never aspire to. There are many great shoots with unimpressive owners, but whoever heard of a great shoot without a great keeper? We owe them our sport and a host of happy memories.

17

PERCH IN THE BUSH

IT HAS BECOME conventional wisdom in snootier circles to claim that Kenya is a busted flush for holidays: Malindi is full of Germans, you can't see the lions in the Mara over the Japanese tour buses and so on. But that is no different from saying that it is no fun going stalking in Sutherland any more because Windsor is full of French backpackers. Kenya is an enormous country. If you want to go where other people are not then it is still marvellously easy to do so.

It is a good start to leave out Nairobi altogether. Once upon a time, most of us used to hanker for the odd night in the old Norfolk Hotel, but nowadays the capital has no more atmosphere than Milton Keynes and rather more crime. Instead, you can nip off the overnight flight from London and head straight for the bush. With reasonable luck, you can be at a lodge far out in the sticks, savouring the perfect Kenyan weather, in time for a shower before lunch.

We paid a first visit to Richard Bonham's wonderful Ol Donyo Wuas, in the Chyulu Hills an hour south-east of Nairobi. Richard, a delightful forty-something Kenyan who is utterly committed to the country and its wildlife, has an exclusive lease from the Masai over 250,000 acres. He has created a little cluster of thatched cottages with a perfect view across the bush to Kilimanjaro, from which one can be taken driving, walking, riding or bird-shooting, more or less wherever you want to go.

I love giraffes, of which there are scores within a few miles of the lodge, along with many other Kenyan species of game. We missed the lions and the rhinos but saw cheetah and their young, together with a host of zebra, all kinds of antelope – including hartebeest – jackals and the rest. Elephants only come that way in the rainy season, but the wonderful loneliness and beauty of the place, and the Bonhams' enthusiasm, made up for any missing animals. Even an hour's drive in an open Land Rover through the chronic dust of Africa was worth it for the view from the top of a hundred-foot kopje in the fading dusk.

An American couple took exception to the cobra in their cottage. I told them that in Botswana a few years ago, my children complained bitterly that only one of them got to see the snake in the loo. They should think themselves very lucky. We rode out every morning, rather to the dismay of the former racehorse that had to carry more than fifteen stone of me, and we enjoyed one of those wonderful bush picnic breakfasts under the acacias.

The smell of woodsmoke, the gentle murmur of African voices in the background, the sudden sunset followed almost instantly by the rise of a clear, sharp full moon are inimitable. If one wanted to niggle, the only downside of Ol Donyo Wuas is that since every gallon of water has to be trucked up from the valley, hot showering is politely rationed. As in almost every lodge, visitors take pot luck with each other's company at meals. That was no hardship for anyone here, unless they happened to hate editors, in which case they were too civil to say so. Drinking whisky and soda outside our perfect cottage on stilts on a perfect evening, I thought that this was as near as one could get to the ideal African experience – and it's a lot less flying time from Heathrow than Zimbabwe, Botswana or Namibia.

We moved on to Lake Victoria. These days, everybody is growing accustomed to being denounced for pursuing the beasts of the field and even the fishes of the sea. What a glow of virtue one feels, therefore, in setting forth to catch a fish which every right-thinking environmentalist has declared must be harried to extinction in the interests of nature.

Twenty or so years ago, some bright spark looking out at Lake Victoria thought what fun it would be to drop in a few Nile perch and see what happened. After all, it is only by a minor accident – the height of Owen Falls – that the vast perch has not got into Victoria on its own. To tip some into the lake would give nature a friendly prod. In the event, as always happens in these cases (see grey squirrels, coypu, mink and other friends of the British animal rights movement), the Nile perch has inflicted upon Lake Victoria an ecological disaster of epic proportions. Once in the water, it chainsawed through every existing species within reach, devouring irresistibly and growing very fat indeed on the proceeds. Today, perch weighing hundreds of pounds roam Lake Victoria. Unless the whole tribe can be wiped out, the ecological diversity of that peerless tract of water will be reduced to a monoculture within a generation.

Thus, sporting reader, anybody who can spare a break from game watching in the Masai Mara and fly down to the Rusinga Island Club for a day or two pursuing Nile perch is performing a public service. Nobody ever says quite that when you head for beat one on the Helmsdale, do they? The Rusinga Club is a cluster of thatched cottages at the north-east corner of the vast water system, which guests share with substantial numbers of lake flies — a non-biting but rather tiresome local phenomenon, whose frequency of appearance in the soup would make H. M. Bateman feel jaded. I turned up at the same time as a Japanese film crew from one of their notorious 'torture' television programmes. They had come to catch a load of lake flies and film one of their screen participants eating them. It would have seemed tasteless to make jokes about the Naked Island, so I suppressed the thought and the flies.

After a good dinner and a view of the long string of local fishermen's lights bobbing far across the water in the darkness, we fell asleep with the grunting of the hippos and woke to the beauty of the morning glory trailing over the tree on the lawn. Philemon Oisma, our boat captain, was a delight. A cheerful, endlessly curious 28-year-old, one of thirteen children of a local farmer, he had recently returned to Rusinga after two years as a fishing guide off Mombasa. Birds were his passion. As we cruised along the lake shore amid the endless profusion of varieties, he identified them and their habits unhesitatingly — kites, kingfishers, herons, egrets, raptors.

We passed an island where the trees were white with the droppings of the great flocks of cormorants and ibises perching on them. Philemon whistled loudly and threw a fish for a sea eagle, which swooped gloriously alongside. 'If you don't feed the eagle, he'll go somewhere else,' he said. 'And I love the eagle best of all birds.'

We bucketed across the north end of the lake before Philemon cut the power, forty yards offshore. Then we ran out the lines – short for the middle rod, long for the port, longer still for the starboard – and began to troll along the lake, exchanging waves with the small boys and girls trailing their poles and lines in the water a gunshot or so distant. Within five minutes, one of the reels shrieked. Philemon cut the engines and wound in the other lines, while I took the bent rod in hand and retrieved hard. On the end was our first very small, very ugly Nile perch – maybe 3lb – very acceptable, but some way short of the 191lb record for rod and line out of Rusinga Island. 'My biggest yet is ninety-two pounds,' said Philemon. 'Last week.' We got back to work.

Pickings were slim that first day. There were a good many false alarms, as the big six-inch lures snagged nets or lines on the bottom, making our senses race with the reels for a few seconds. We lost a couple of fish, too – on and off almost as soon as I had taken up the rod. But the weather was perfect, as Kenyan weather almost always is. I was enchanted by Philemon's intelligent curiosity about almost every aspect of the world. He seized the bird book in excitement when he spotted a tern he had not seen before, then returned to quizzing me closely about the letting arrangements for Scottish salmon fishing.

The echo sounder was blipping constantly – perch seem to take best in fifteen to twenty feet of water. As we belted back across the lake, the afternoon breeze had risen, creating

conditions resembling a moderate chop in the English
Channel. Suddenly, we understood the reasons for the oil-
skins in the locker. Next morning the weather was perfect
again and flat calm. Philemon sternly discouraged feminine
proposals for swimming offshore, on the grounds that the
crocodiles would not approve. We started trolling again.
This time, we were quickly into fish – perch of 10lb, 5lb,
17lb – big enough to give a serious pull on the line, half
a dozen in all and a respectable morning's haul, even if
modest by Nile perch standards.

It is Africa, rather than the fish, which is the focus of
an outing like this one – the cormorants, scorning the boat's
best, speed to race past us, the peerless sunset with the hills
behind, the lateen sails of the fishing boats and their
cheerful crews, the thatched huts and weavers' nests along
the shoreline, the hills dripping lush tropical greenery
which rise sheer from the waterside in places, creating a
backdrop for the graceful ibises.

'Time to call it a day, I think,' said Philemon, whose
grasp of English vernacular was irresistible. I wouldn't mind
much if I didn't see a Nile perch again, except on the table.
But the company of such a boatman is among the greatest
joys of sport.

18

Uncle Lewis

We were talking the other day about big game, and about people who pay thousands of pounds for licences to kill elephant, lion, giraffe. If the money is ploughed back into conservation – a big 'if' in Africa – and some species are overstocked in a given area, there seems nothing wrong with the principle of reviving some big-game hunting. Yet many of us still feel uncomfortable about it.

What sort of sportsmen nowadays gain satisfaction from firing a very heavy bullet at a very large animal? All personal opinions on this subject are irrational, of course. My own is founded upon the belief that killing a pheasant or a

grouse is a matter of cropping the surplus of a plentiful
species, while I couldn't shoot something as awesome as an
elephant for pleasure. Any opponent of field sports would
snort at such muddled thinking, and declare that there
is no moral difference between killing one species for
pleasure and another. I disagree. Large creatures are generally more rare than small ones. Our forebears, however, were
untroubled. I grew up with special respect for my Great-
Uncle Lewis – aka Major Lewis Hastings, MC, b.1880 –
who devoted much of his life to demolishing African wildlife during those frustrating periods when there was a close
season on Germans and he wasn't in the mood for writing
poetry.

The family archive is stuffed with pictures of Lewis in
the approved style of the period, standing with a foot on
various large corpses. He was also a trenchant and wonderfully politically incorrect writer. One of his *bon mots*
appeared for some years in a dictionary of modern quo-
tations, only to be summarily deleted in a more enlightened
age. 'A lot of nonsense is talked about freedoms in Africa,'
he wrote. 'Freedom of speech, freedom of thought and so
on. The only freedom Africans really care about is freedom
from trousers.' You see what I mean? To the end of his life,
he continued to believe – as did my father – that Africa
south of the Zambesi both should and would remain white-
dominated. But I have always thought some of his prose on
the pre-1914 days in Africa worthy of Karen Blixen. As a
hunter far from civilization, he wrote: 'You hear more –
you see things, you see more of them and you see further.
That heightened sensibility to external impressions which
shepherds have, and gamekeepers and gardeners and hunters
– that's one of the chief rewards. Awareness of movement
and growth and seasonal signs, of footprints in the dust, of

wind and the stars – those are the things that are blunted by books.'

He described Mafuta, his gunbearer, a veteran of the King's African Rifles, waking him at dawn in the bush: ' "Good morning, *n'kosi*. Klass has cleaned the shotgun and gone out to get some guinea fowl. The elephants went over the river into the reed bed last night. The *n'tombi* has come from the village with some eggs. A hyena has come in the night and taken a buffalo hide. The sugar is finished."

'So there you were – all the real news in headlines. But Mafuta always put the good news first and the bad last, which is a much better idea than the one current in Fleet Street.'

Lewis and his generation were sportsmen of a toughness almost unknown today, whose experiences in pursuit of game make any challenges which a modern generation undertakes seem slight. One day, alone in the bush, when desperately short of meat for the pot, Lewis took a long-range snap shot at an antelope. He was delighted to find it lying apparently stone dead in the grass. But as he bent down to start skinning the beast, it sprang to life. It had only been grazed by Lewis's bullet: 'I threw myself on him, and grabbed him by the throat, dropping my knife as I did so. The next second his razor-sharp hooves cut clean through my belt, just missing the skin. Many and many a time I'd handled calves for branding, but this thing was like a bundle of steel springs. I twisted my legs round him and bore down as hard as I could. My weight was 190lb, and the bushbuck was no more than 90, but it took everything I had to hang on and to prevent his hooves ripping me to pieces.

'At last I managed to shift the grip from the throat to his horns, and with that additional leverage I wriggled him round underneath me until I could reach my knife. Even after I had opened it with my teeth, the buck nearly broke from me and I had to hold on again. All this time he was blowing foam in my face, his tongue was lolling out of the corner of his mouth, and he was making the fiercest kind of ram noises. But I got him where I wanted him in the end, drove the knife in and cut his windpipe.

'For quite some little time I sat down after this struggle covered with blood, which was mostly the buck's. Then I tore my tattered shirt into strips, tied one strip round my torn shorts, and fastened the antelope's legs together with the other. I dragged the heavy body over my shoulders and started back for the camp.' Makes stalking seem undemanding, doesn't it?

Lewis described walking thirty miles in a day, hunting elephant, setting out before dawn when it was so cold 'the rifle barrel seemed to burn your fingers'. He wrote of pursuing antelope from the saddle: 'The nearest waiting horseman gallops for all he is worth, not towards the pack but across the line in front of them. Hardly checking from the gallop he flings the reins on his horse's neck, throws himself off, and firing from the knee picks off one flying buck after another as the multitude run, spring and jink at close quarters . . . We were shooting for a living. Still, Venter and I enjoyed every moment of the chase, and that would probably damn us in the eyes of Bloomsbury.'

A wagon drawn by sixteen oxen took their spoils each weekend down to Kimberley. In his later years, he wrote, 'I found myself less interested in trophies and more in the fun of following and finding birds and animals. That's a natural sequence, and it doesn't imply any self-reproach about actual hunting experiences.'

He was not a bad poet and published several collections. The first appeared during the First World War, when he started his military service as a trooper in the Imperial

Yeomanry during the campaign in German South-West
Africa. In those days, he wrote Kiplingesque doggerel. Most
of his later work extolled the joys of the wild places and
vented his spleen against cities, intellectuals and socialists.
This one dates from around 1934:

Once I saw London from the iron bridge,
Dark London pierced with stars,
Moving stars along the Embankment,
And a thousand still stars in the City's gloom.
I heard the sad hum of the million prisoners,
And the stone-bound earth
       murmuring beneath their million feet.
And then in a heart's beat,
Low and swift over the iron girders,
Wild duck flew seaward!
Out of the night they came
And into the night passed strong and swift.

O wild wings! O little lovely brothers!
The canopy of night parted,
And the clamour of the night-bound city
Vanished in bright mist,
I saw the dawn—
Dawn on the river, the dark river, the dark shining
       river of Africa
Where in a live silence
Flamingoes swing in rosy circles,
And in reedy pools
The crocodile, the everlasting,
Dreams marshy voluptuous dreams
       of long-dead cities
That feel flaming amid the assegais
And stank delectably in the marsh.

My father, who idolized Lewis, did his best to emulate some of his doings in the 1950s, bearing his uncle's old rifles. I still possess a notably horrible ashtray made from the foot of a bison father whacked in India. Though he once shot for the pot when he was crossing the Kalahari, most of the time he killed African game because he enjoyed doing so, and his generation still perceived it as a virile thing to do.

Today's change of mood has come about not only because of the scarcity of many African game species, but also because shooting an elephant no longer seems a convincing demonstration of masculinity. Andrew Fraser's death on the horns of a buffalo recently reminded us how dangerous big animals can be. But most modern shooters in Africa are saved by vehicles from the sort of physical exertion Lewis's generation knew, and their escorting hunters insulate them from much danger.

If you're rich enough to buy the licences to shoot big game, you're also rich enough to make sure you don't have to suffer much to do so. A while ago I was shown the honeymoon snaps of the daughter of a transatlantic billionaire, whose present to the bride was a licence to shoot a sample of every major species of African big game.

Seeing the corpse of a humble buck in the inventory, I said I was surprised she had bothered to waste a bullet: 'Oh, he was just bait for the lion.' She obviously had the time of her life. I am not sure she did anything very demanding. But if she reads this, she might riposte, 'What's the difference between what I did and what you do when you stalk red deer in Scotland?'

Not a lot. It is the skill of the stalker which gets me a stag, rather than any genius on my part in squeezing the trigger. But we can be more confident about the need to reduce the numbers of Scottish red deer than those of African big game. More than twenty years ago, game numbers in Rhodesia got out of hand during the guerrilla war. I was working out there as a correspondent. A park ranger asked me one day if I would like to go out with him and shoot an elephant. I was tempted for a moment, as a gesture to the shades of Uncle Lewis and my father. But without much real hesitation I declined, and have never since regretted the lost opportunity.

The way Africa is going, elephants and other big beasts will be lucky to outlast our lifetimes, save in a few parks. The pressures upon them are overwhelming, reinforced by the belief of many Africans that conservation is a toy created by the rich white man only after he had shot most of the game for himself and lost power over his empires. Tigers and rhinos are in desperate straits worldwide. Firearms have become ubiquitous in both Africa and India, with tragic consequences for wildlife.

Uncle Lewis, writing in 1946, saw it all coming: 'Africa has her secret life, like nothing else on earth . . . but it is going fast . . . The millennium is at hand. In England, soon the pheasant woods will all be cleared for corn, mechanized farming will uproot the hedges, the cathedrals will be turned into industrial flats, and in Africa what remains of the antelope will be penned in well-ordered Whipsnades. Virtue will be compulsory, we will buy all our meat from the butchers, and there will be no more cakes and ale. Hunting, in particular, will be put down with a strong hand by the Security Police.'

The old boy died in 1966. How delighted he must have been not to live to see some of his savagely cynical predictions fulfilled.

19

STAGS IN THE MIST

'IT'S NO GOOD for the high ground today, that's for sure,'
said Peter the stalker, gazing up at the swirling mist which
became impenetrable around 500 feet. We would have to
make the best of it lower down. We set off from close to sea
level, trudging up the steep face above the loch, the rain
eddying around us as we climbed.

I am only an occasional stalker, but most of my memories of days after deer include the wet soaking through to
the inmost recesses of my garments within the first hour.
On the credit side, this October morning wasn't cold, and
Peter gave me an engrossing little lesson through the climb,

about dry-curing ham by use of salt, pepper, juniper berries
and a touch of saltpetre on the bone. When he is not on
the hill he is at his pigs.

The only sadness that morning was his pessimism about
his own art. 'I've loved every moment of it,' he said, 'but I
don't want my son in it. It's a dying business. You've only
got to see the funny looks you get, when you go into
Inverness these days in a suit of tweeds, never mind carrying
a gun case. Scottish National Heritage don't want deer. The
Forestry Commission don't want deer. You can see the way
the wind's blowing that the Forestry have just hired two
stalkers to go all around Scotland shooting deer. If we go
on like this, stalking as we know it will be finished in
twenty years.'

The Forestry Commission contest the truth of the
assertion about their own policy, but the stalker's remarks
reflect his belief. He was also dismayed by the new mood
he perceives towards Scottish land ownership, spurred by
the financial support given to crofters to buy their own
ground on Eigg and at Assynt. 'Now they're saying they
want to make the Cairngorms a "National Park". Once
they start on that, it's all over.' I said that it seemed too
soon to regard the battles as lost. An estate such as the one
we were stalking puts a fortune into conservation and grants
public access in the most generous spirit. There is simply
a long argument to be won.

On top of the cliff, we breasted a knoll and found
ourselves with a misty view across broken ground for a mile
or so in all directions. Each of a hundred ridges and burn
bottoms could hide deer. We advanced cautiously, peering
delicately over each little face, stopping to spy in the murky
grey light. After another half-hour's walking we lay down
for a long, hard look.

It took ten minutes' intent scrutiny for Peter to spot a

stag and three hinds in shelter 700 yards or so eastwards. I
had to say honestly that even with my cherished 8 × 56
Zeiss glasses, I could have studied the hill all morning
without seeing those deer. But that is what the art of the
professional stalker is all about.

Good old Stonehenge, writing in 1875, proclaimed that,
'a hardy frame and plenty of pluck,' are needed for stalking,
adding that, 'the foot should be sure and the eye keen and
long seeing . . . Great control over the feelings is absolutely
essential; for the giving way to the exultation of hope or
the depression produced by the fear of the loss of a shot,
will generally cause that which is most to be apprehended.'
Nonetheless, even in those days, after cataloguing all these
wonderful virtues the rifle should profess, the writer added
somewhat lamely, 'Most deer stalkers content themselves
with obeying the directions of their gillies, and when these
men know what is wanted of them, they generally contrive
to suit the stalker.' Quite. Stonehenge would be disgusted
by the physical condition of most modern rifles, and rendered speechless by the Argocat. The truth is, I am afraid,
that one reason for the steep decline, in real money, of the
cost of deerstalking, as against other forms of field sports
in modern times against Victorian days, is that relatively
few modern sportsmen are prepared to do the work inseparable even from following a 'gillie' up the hill to shoot a
stag.

Still we stayed put on that hillside, waiting and listening. 'There's another stag roaring much nearer to us, and
I want to be sure where he is,' said my companion. We lay
and watched and listened. A stag and hinds on the northern
hill face began loping upwards into thick mist. They
shouldn't have winded us. 'But the trouble is up here, the
wind goes round and round, and you can never tell,' said
Peter.

After another ten minutes, he decided we should cross the steep burn bottom below us, then work up the opposite face for a look at the deer eastwards. 'Mind now, I can't promise there's anything shootable, but that stag looked to have a very grey face.' We clambered down the scree and over the burn, sheltered for a while from the fierce head-wind. Peter gestured at my stick, tapping on a rock. I hastily shouldered it.

A sceptical female companion once asked where my skill came into stalking, as distinct from that of the stalker. In truth, we all know that every stag is the stalker's achievement. For the rifle, the joy lies in learning to keep faith with the oldest principles of hunting and fieldcraft, for which a modern pavement generation has lost its instinct. That, and the sort of hill walk which tests middle-age legs. At least this morning I wasn't pouring sweat, as so often on a sunlit August day.

A quarter of an hour on, I was lying on the edge of the hill, gazing down at the big old stag, brilliantly lit through my 'scope sight. God, when I think of the years I was stupid enough to stalk with a cheap sight, and of the stalker's time I wasted doing so. In poor light I could scarcely see a beast, never mind shoot it. Now, with a bipod and my piece of Austrian optical wizardry, at 200 yards I knew it would be hard to make a mess of things.

The stag was lying down. 'I'm going to try and get him up,' said Peter. He rolled on his side and roared. The stag threw his head forward and roared in response. Four, five times stalker and beast roared at each other while I lay over the eyepiece, completely gripped. The stag lumbered to his feet and stood for a second to give me a perfect shot.

He turned and staggered when I fired. I cursed as I ejected the spent case and rammed another clinking round into the chamber. 'Don't shoot again! Don't shoot again!'

said Peter. 'He's down.' The beast fell forward on the hill and rolled over dead. A few moments later we were standing over him. 'Only six points, but what a head!' said the stalker. 'He's eighteen stone, anyway. Think of what he must have been!'

They scorn radios or Argocats in that forest. The stalker slipped away across the hill to get the ponies, and I sat musing beside my flask and the dead beast in the rain. The dreaded health police are putting ever more pressure on deer forests, with helpful suggestions that stalkers should sterilize their knives, and take a shovel to the hill to bury the gralloch. 'And who do they think is to tell the foxes not to dig it up?' as Peter enquired sardonically.

An hour or two later, I was watching one of those wonderful grey garrons step carefully over the rocks with the stag lurching on its saddle and reflecting that, even in the mist and the shimmering rain, this was one of the most romantic sights in Scotland. If any field sport deserves to outlive us all, it is deerstalking.

It is hardest to argue with those critics who think it is wrong to allow anyone to gain pleasure from killing, that even if the deer must be culled, professionals should do the business. Those of us who go to the hill, however, believe to the bottom of our hearts that to stalk, to hunt across the high tops, enables us to touch one of the deepest and healthiest human instincts of all.

20

WHAT IT IS TO 'GO WELL'

IN THE FOX-HUNTING counties the pace of life, both vertical and horizontal, has been ordered for centuries by the goings-on of the hunting hearties. In recent memory they have been smashing up each others' Range Rovers, overturning Lincolnshire dinner tables, punching each other behind hedges at the meet, as part of the immemorial mating ritual of the lesser thick-headed Shires swell. Some of the silliest men in England, to the rage of less well-endowed rivals, have been able to play like lutes upon the affections of some of the prettiest women, merely on the grounds that they can get over a few fences without breaking their half-witted necks.

Yes, well, by now fox-hunters are saying that they can see exactly where Hastings is coming from – and that jealousy will get him nowhere. But it remains a remarkable fact of British life in the last days of the twentieth century that at dinner in Leicestershire one can listen to a man being done over for beating his wife, pawning his mother's jewellery, passing dud cheques and breaking his stepchildren's trust funds – only to find absolution being offered in the last reverent sentence: 'But doesn't he *go well?*'

In a post-fox-hunting era, what would be the fate of those celebrated Masters and followers, whose claims upon the attentions of so many women rest entirely upon their prowess in pursuit of foxes? Would proven skill in chasing a drag confer the same charms? Would the ability to talk intelligently about Mozart, to flatter a woman of a certain age about her looks, come anywhere to matching the appeal to girls of a man in a pink coat who crosses country as if he means business? Having listened over the years to a remarkable amount of gay chatter about the sexual misalliances of the fox-hunting world, I still find myself cross-questioning experts on these matters with the fascination Darwin must have experienced when he first saw giant turtles going at it on the Galapagos.

Are hunting relationships ever, or even often – I ask – consummated in the field? I cherish a print on the wall of my own home which I inherited from my father, entitled *The Belle of the Hunt*. This depicts a Victorian beauty allegedly kissing her beau as they gallop side by side in mid-run. The image is charming, but the practical difficulties would be enormous. And surely even the most energetic Quorn types could scarcely go the whole hog in the saddle?

Experts assure me that it is, in truth, far too cold to attempt consummation on a hunting day with even the doughtiest 'goer'. What would one do with the horses?

And, even for aspiring Eskimos, there always seem to be foot followers peering from every bush. 'It's hard enough to find cover behind which to go to the loo,' a devoted hunting woman mutters to me, 'never mind go to the Master.'

But plenty of horseboxes have apparently been abused for reproductive, or at least copulatory, purposes. I was shocked to hear this. I have always understood that there is an admirable rural saying: 'Don't do it where you'll frighten the horses.' What was it Lord Chesterfield said? 'The pleasure is transitory, the expense damnable, and the position ridiculous.' But I suppose one can train one's hunter to overcome its natural disgust about anything.

It sometimes seems that all conversation in the Shires would come to a halt without the antics of a handful of legendary mounted bonkers to keep everybody gossiping. An exceptionally rich and beautiful girl has proved a staple of dinner-party chat for twenty years and more. Until recently, the common denominator of her men was that they 'went well'. In middle age she has changed tack and settled down to life with a not notably bright ex-cavalry officer, a decade or two younger than herself. Maybe Army equitation courses aren't what they used to be. However splendid the horses she finds for this young lad, it seems that he doesn't ride too well and keeps falling off.

There was a memorable day out with – no, let's say the Blankshire – when somebody cantered up to this girl's usual place at the front of the field, and shouted, with a weary gesture of the thumb over his shoulder, 'You'd better get back there and do something, Sally. Your baby's fallen out of his pram again!'

Another red-blooded female follower became so seized with enthusiasm for a local equestrian hero that she rang his doorbell late one night. When he answered, she dropped her fur coat to reveal herself – well, more or less in the

state of a hunter without its rug. Not only did the cad ask
her in, he dined out on the story for years afterwards,
somewhat to the irritation of the siren's husband.

A double-barrelled Shires Master is alleged to have set
off for the meet, absent-mindedly leaving two women hand-
cuffed to his banisters. He enjoyed an excellent day and
returned to find his little *mise-en-scène* unchanged since
breakfast. History does not record whether this lively tri-
angular relationship survived the experience. Some while
ago now, one of Leicestershire's leading mounted bounders
went too far by half, and was found by his stepchildren
drunk and unconscious on the sitting-room floor having
been most disagreeable to his wife before he passed out.
The steps tied him up, carried him to the boot of their car
and drove him thirty miles to his mother's house, where
they left him in bondage on the doorstep at 2 a.m. He was
not seen again before the divorce. Today, he is said to be
still hunting shamelessly in both vertical and horizontal
modes, but has had to be fired and keeps having a problem
with over-reaching.

Now, when I put pen to paper to record these racy tales,
my fox-hunting friends are enraged. I am giving a wholly
false picture of hunting social life, they say. Oh, all right,
under duress they admit that it may not be a *false* picture,
but they claim that it is a highly damaging one, which
diminishes the dignity and respectability of their sport.
Nothing is further from my intentions. We should be a
poorer and greyer society if fox-hunting was taken from us,
not because the foxes would mind, but because the humans
would have so much less to talk about in rural circles,
without fox-hunters doing it upside down swinging from
the chandeliers. Nothing comparable seems to happen to
shooters and fishers. Can you imagine what people would
say if one decamped into a wood behind the line with a

woman on a good driven-pheasant day? Two very small people might just about manage something in a grouse butt; only at the cost of infinite shaking of heads and cross mutterings about couples who can't get their priorities straight. So confusing for the pickers-up, too.

There are days, even weeks, on Scottish salmon rivers when one is more usefully employed dallying with the other sex than casting a fly – during a serious drought or when there is direct sunlight on the pool. But the rest of the time, the only purpose for which a sensible fisherman could ask a woman to undress would be to secure fly-tying materials of the kind so vividly described in the *Field*'s correspondence column a while ago. To spare any sensitive blushes here, let us just explain that the technique involves a pair of scissors and access to an accommodating woman somewhere between the waist and the knee, together with a fly vice. But this has absolutely nothing to do with sex, to which serious pursuers of salmon are properly indifferent, and everything to do with catching fish.

No, I fear fox-hunters are unique among field sportsmen in their preoccupation with fornication, a phenomenon which seems irredeemably identified with the equestrian lifestyle. If the new puritans got their way and it all stopped, there would be nothing for the wilder wing of the hunting fraternity to look forward to, save a great many cold baths.

21

LAST POST FOR THE MAJORS

A FEW MONTHS ago, driving between stands at a shoot and reflecting on the usual clutter of kit strewn around the vehicle, I was gazing at the Brigade of Guards strap on my neighbour's cartridge bag. 'Where were you?' I asked. 'Irish Guards tanks, Guards Armoured Division,' he replied briefly. Because I write military history books, I am probably one of the few people of my age who could thus place him in the Norman cornfields in August 1944.

For years, the amusing little conceit of the Brigade cartridge bag has been part of the shooting scene. Likewise there was a time, say thirty years ago, when, if you had called out 'Major!' in the middle of any driven shoot, two or three men would inevitably have looked up. Today, we see far fewer of them. Over the next decade or two, actuarially, they will become almost extinct.

An entire generation of sportsmen either served for a few years in their youth in the war or did National Service. But the youngest veterans of National Service are now approaching sixty. Each year Britain becomes a more civilian society, happily for our generation without experience of war or military life. On the river and in the shooting field the gradual waning of the old soldiers diminishes the social colour of the scene. All of us have encountered so many of those ageing colonels and majors, who seemed to have been – and often were – born with a gun under their arm or a saddle between their knees.

In the immediate post-war years even some former captains clung to their ranks. This was widely perceived as ridiculous everywhere outside Northern Ireland, where no man could get anywhere in local politics unless he could prove a captaincy in a reputable regiment. Terence O'Neill still called himself captain when he was Northern Ireland prime minister in the late 1960s.

In England and Scotland, no group of guns seemed able to foregather without a field officer or two present. As one whose dress often attracted unfavourable attention in the line, I remember from an early age quailing beneath the sardonic looks of assorted veterans, men of punctilious appearance even in retirement. Deprived of a batman to supply the elbow grease, they still brought their brown brogues to a preternatural shine. If they no longer wore pips on their shoulders, they retained a tightly trimmed moustache as a badge of rank and flinched visibly at breaches of etiquette, unless executed by themselves. Incorrect form of any kind caused them physical pain, above all attempts to count things – cartridges, pheasants, personal scores. J. K. Stanford was perhaps their vicar on earth, reflecting in his lividly intolerant prose the old cavalryman's horror of an urban aesthete or a rural bounder.

Most were, of course, almost entirely deaf, to the despair of those who had to live with them. In their day it was thought incorrigibly wet to stuff four-by-two in one's ears, merely because of close proximity to artillery barrages or machine-gun fire. By the age of forty they could hear only summonses to eat or drink, and orders delivered at parade-ground volume. Heaven knows how the many mistresses of the hunting ones conversed with their men at all, other than with the aid of a horn. Some soldiers wrote wryly witty sporting memoirs, like Major Jarvis. But most were not great readers of anything much save rural magazines and Surtees. They thought of Evelyn Waugh simply as that frightful little shit who should never have got a commission. I would never have dared knowingly appear at a shoot or on a river-bank without a tie on a day a Brigade cartridge bag or two was likely to be in evidence. They took sporting matters immensely seriously. When writing a book about the Korean War, I came upon the orders issued by the colonel of the 8th Hussars before their embarkation for a journey which culminated in the bloody showdown on the Imjin in April 1951. These included the memorable instruction: 'Take a gun, but not your *best* gun.' None of his subordinates, I am sure, for a moment supposed that their commanding officer was discussing tank armament.

As we become a less military society, a lot of the nuances of veterans' conversation are lost on a new generation. When a former soldier tells another at lunch that he came out only as a lieutenant-colonel, 'but I commanded the regiment before I left', then his companion knows exactly how dearly this matters, in a way that a lifelong civilian does not.

One day on a moor in Yorkshire, I was chatting to a recently retired officer. Guessing his age, I asked if he had retired as a colonel. 'No,' he replied sadly. 'I was the oldest major in the Brigade of Guards. When the last chance for a step came, and there were two of us eligible, they said the other chap had better have it, because I had a private income and he didn't.'

How much poorer conversation on the hill and the river will become when the scope for such gems has faded, and we hear only of property deals and bonuses. Like the rest of us, some of those old soldiers were nice men, others were monsters; some shot straight, some did not. But they possessed a common denominator: they were unmistakably forged and shaped – some might say in a narrow mould – by the experience of war, and by seeing and doing things of which few of our generation have any understanding.

Many of them consciously sought to represent that much-derided duality, an officer and a gentleman. Their efforts in this department deserve more respect than they are sometimes given. We should enjoy the survivors while there are still some around us, because we shall miss them when they are gone.

22

FIRST SLICE YOUR CHAINSAW

As I HUNG precariously from a ladder in my garden one day, breaking every rule of chainsaw safety, decapitating a thick hedge two feet above my head by holding the lethal weapon at full-arm stretch, I pondered the passion of almost all men for garden machines. I have a friend in Yorkshire who in outward appearance is the most sober of fifty-something-year-old lawyers as well as general good blokes. A few years ago this chap fell off a ladder with a chainsaw on top of him which he had carelessly omitted to switch off. To cut a long story short, he covered 300 yards to his house and two miles to the local hospital just in time to avoid bleeding to death. He spent months in painful rehabilitation, and bits of him have never been quite the same since. A couple of years later, I was shooting as his guest. Remembering that he had recently bought a new Suzuki jeep, I asked where it was. He blushed more deeply than he does at the mention of any woman's name and muttered something about a tree falling on it.

'No, no, NO!' I shrieked. 'You couldn't have done! Not a chainsaw again?' He nodded mutely. Now, in civilian life I would consider my Yorkshire friend to be the steadiest citizen I could name, a man to go tiger-shooting with, or to whom to entrust one's infant children. But put a garden machine of any kind into his hands and this paragon becomes transformed into a dangerous maniac.

I might find this hard to understand, was I not familiar with the same problem in my own family. My father, Macdonald Hastings, forty years ago a celebrated country writer and broadcaster, possessed a passion for garden machinery that in a less charitable age would have caused him to be confined. Where lesser gardeners prodded plants with a hoe, weeded with a hand trowel or dug a border with a mere garden fork, Father believed that every horticultural task was susceptible to a violent mechanical solution. He wasted a fortune over the years on buying new labour-saving wheelbarrows, patent pruners, non-strain forks, automatic compost-makers. His faith in all of them was short-lived. Scrap merchants found it profitable to visit the graveyard of these splendid innovations at the bottom of the garden a few months after purchase. But failure never discouraged Father's persistence in searching for a horticultural Holy Grail. He was convinced that, given money and determination, means could be found to divorce gardening from manual labour.

Broadcasters and writers have more scope than most people for exploring their own fantasies. Product manufacturers hungry for publicity will assist. One day in about 1960, Father decided to get a lot of gardening done extremely cheaply at our extravagantly neglected cottage garden in Berkshire. He evolved a plan to do a 'dream' film for BBC TV's old *Tonight* programme in which he stood musing about a magic transformation of his garden, and lo – a legion of machines swept up the path to sort out his garden at the wave of a wand.

The manufacturers cooperated enthusiastically with this wheeze. On the appointed day, amid a crowd of fascinated spectators, the old Newman camera rolled. Father stood centre stage in white flannels. Towards him powered all the machines which garden science was then capable of unleashing. There were flame-throwers and mowers, rotavators in profusion, weeders and diggers, pruners and sprayers and hedge clippers, and even a man with something called a Killer Kane, with which he walked along poking weeds to deadly effect.

Each of these infernal machines and its keeper selected a corner of our modest acre and roared away. It was a startling sight which I observed from a distance, aged thirteen or so, because I was sulking over the fact that my sister was given a cameo role in the film while I was not. My mother, a serious gardener, absented herself from the holocaust altogether. All through the daylight hours, the noisy juggernauts tilled and harrowed, scorched and turned, until scarcely a buttercup dared lift its head, never mind more cultured species.

At close of play, the armoured column rolled away on its transporters. We were left once more in tranquil possession of the field. The film was a great success. One of Father's greatest attributes, which contributed mightily to

his success as a television presenter, was that his barmiest
beliefs were quite untinged with scepticism. Each time he
embraced a new enthusiasm, he did so with the faith of a
true believer. He could persuade all but the most rational
viewers to do likewise.

But the lesson of the mechanical dream experience,
which any sane gardener could have taught Father before
he started, was that while machinery can flatten the landscape, it cannot make things grow. Our rustic acre was
reduced to a superbly tilled and incinerated wasteland. Of
flowers, shrubs and vegetables only an archaeologist could
have discovered a trace.

Since Father failed to embark upon any follow-up
process of his own, the garden quickly reverted to a jungle
until, years later, my mother replanted it all. The only
legacy of the Great Gardening Dream was a pile of decaying
machinery in the garage, which Father bought at a discount
from the manufacturers and never used. I was grateful for
the flame-thrower, which proved a stimulating instrument
for teenage experiment. And yes, my eyebrows grew back
quite quickly, thank you.

Today, looking back on it all, I suppose my own philosophy – that there is no garden problem which cannot be
solved by either a JCB or a chainsaw – owes much to
that early indoctrination. My former colleague at the *Daily
Telegraph*, the great Lord Deedes, owns no less than three
chainsaws. I have always considered Bill a remarkably gentle
and good-natured man, yet his enthusiasm for lethal
machinery echoes that of my Yorkshire friend whom I
mentioned at the outset. These things bring out the Jekyll
and Hyde contrast in us all, the lurking beast. I used to
prune tenderly with secateurs, but having discovered the
merits of addressing roses with a hedge trimmer, hardly a

leaf is left by the time I have finished when the mechanical fever is upon me.

If Father were alive today he would regard subsidiary modern implements such as the strimmer and hedge trimmer as mere flutes in the great orchestra of automated gardening, alongside the heavy metal of excavators, ride-on tractors and chainsaws. I am not alone among male gardeners in being prone to forget names of plants and even rather common shrubs. But the most absent-minded man remembers the brand names of his tools, and spends quite as much time poring over machinery handbooks as more sensitive souls, usually female, devote to seed catalogues. I have never much believed in spiritualism. But if I could find a good medium, I am convinced that no temporal intelligence would more excite Father, wherever he may be today, than to learn of the invention of a self-propelled mulcher.

23

SEEING OFF BENJAMIN BUNNY

UNTIL RECENTLY I can't say that rabbits have played a big part in my life. When I was a Bloodthirsty Young Thing, like most BYTs, I spent happy hours pursuing furry nuisances by night in the headlights of a Land Rover. But in our part of the world we had to quest far afield to find any. Those were the days when myxie seemed to have laid them low for good. Many a country columnist in the 1960s and 1970s wrote nostalgic pieces lamenting the disappearance of those charming rural activities which called for warreners and ferrets.

The urban public likes bunnies for the same reasons that it warms to seals and foxes. They are furry, cuddly and go hoppity hoppity through the pages of many a charming children's book. Even allowing for Peter Rabbit, Beatrix Potter adopted a sensibly unsentimental approach to the species and made plain her view that their natural destiny lay in a pot. Kenneth Grahame, whose insidious PR work for water rats and moles has caused generations of children to spring traps on the sly ever since, portrayed rabbits as merely silly. But then along came Richard Adams with that damnable book, *Watership Down*, which encouraged the notion of rabbits as philosophers and moral giants, stirring the passions of an entire generation of those who have never seen what a philosophical rabbit or two can do to a young plantation.

My own troubles with dear little Benjamin Bunny started when I bought a new house in west Berkshire and was doing some major surgery on the garden. The landscaper working on my borders rang me in London one morning. 'You know you've got rabbits?' he said. 'They're doing terrible things to your roses.' No, I didn't know. Ridiculously unobservant though the admission made me sound, I had been too busy working on the house during the winter to spot the furry curse outside.

It was a hard freeze which brought them brutally to notice. Those eighty roses, which I had spent so many hours planting with my own fair hands, were being chewed to bits. As an emergency measure we fenced the beds, while I set about organizing a more serious counter-offensive. Once I started looking out for bunnies, it was not difficult to knock off a few of the more feckless, though even this has become a cumbersome affair. When most of us were young country dwellers a rook rifle lived by the back door for the summary disposal of vermin. Nowadays, after you spot your rabbit, you've got to find the keys of the gun cabinet, unlock gun and ammunition, study subsection iii (para 12) of your Firearms Certificate and make sure your neighbourhood RSPB representative isn't crawling about in the bushes protecting the local goshawk. By the time you engage a bunny in your sights, it has died at a venerable old age laden with honours, after producing several flourishing families.

Rabbits, like crows, always know when you have a gun. I kept meeting them round corners every time I was armed with nothing more lethal than a garden fork. They vanished for a week to the Caribbean each time I went looking for them with malice aforethought. I soon reached the conclusion which any experienced rabbit bopper would have attained at the outset: shooting rabbits is an agreeable amusement for BYTs but contributes next to nothing to dealing with them as a horticultural menace.

Innocently, I assumed that it would be a pretty simple matter to find somebody else to deal with my plague. Yet rabbit controllers are harder to come by than of yore. My landscaper said he thought he had seen someone advertise in the *Newbury Weekly News*. I scanned the small ads studiously but couldn't see anything useful. I rang the local keeper. He couldn't offer any suggestions. There were so many rabbits about, he said. People didn't like using their ferrets when there were so many young in the buries. It was such a performance getting gas, signing the Poison Book and so on.

One sunny afternoon, driving round the lanes to my house, I saw rabbits everywhere: twenty or more in the small field adjoining the garden; several on the road beyond; a couple even scurrying along the tarmac in the neighbouring farmyard. Okay, no more argument: I needed to take drastic action. A week later a fencing specialist had dug 300 metres of rabbit netting around the entire vulnerable side of my garden. The cost made me whiten. But what choice was there? A friend who is also a keen gardener told me cheerfully that before she wired her place at hideous expense, 'the rabbits simply grazed the borders'. Having just planted heaven knows how many hundred young plants, I was damned if I would surrender the beds to become the local Watership Down.

There remained a very small spinney inside my boundary, a mere 50 yards by 10. A friend provided a canister of gas capsules. I spent a Saturday afternoon crawling on hands and knees through the bushes and brambles in my gardening gloves, poking capsules down every bury, while my fourteen-year-old son followed behind with a spade, filling the holes. 'Couldn't we leave just one, Daddy?' he pleaded. I was momentarily bemused by this outbreak of sentiment until he added wistfully, 'So we still have some to shoot.' No, we jolly well could not. To my astonishment, in that tiny area I identified twenty-nine holes. Whenever I have a spare moment, I crawl through the spinney again, on relentless patrol in search of more cuddly, furry things. I could have built a new kitchen for not much more than the fencing cost. But the rabbit peril has become an obsession.

Now, to be serious for a moment, I suppose one should be grateful that in the case of rabbits, whether the public likes them or not, not even Elliot Morley seriously suggests – yet, anyway – that we should be prevented from killing them. But my little difficulties have redoubled my sympathy for people who are plagued by badgers or seals. As we all know, if your garden or paddock is being devastated by badgers and you try to do anything lethal about it, the full weight of the law will descend. If there is trouble with cormorants or hen harriers, there is no choice save to offer them some more lunch, unless one wants to be publicly denounced by the RSPB. And if the estuary of your salmon river is serving as the Savoy Grill for a football crowd of grey seals, well, tough. You can't fence the Helmsdale or the Spey.

But the rabbit problem has plainly become widespread once more, and is likely to cause plenty of grief yet. Half the county, and many other counties besides, are discussing what can be done about this, a problem few country-dwellers have had to consider for twenty years. Many of a new generation have convinced themselves that rabbits have rights, too, that they deserve to be left in peace. One afternoon I was driving my son and a fellow teenager up to the teenager's father's house. Along his drive, we passed a rabbit tribe grazing happily among the bushes. 'Daddy! Daddy!' said my offspring eagerly, 'can't we go home and get the rifle?' St Francis, or whatever our young host was called, dropped his jaw in horror. 'You can't shoot the rabbits. Those are *our* rabbits!' he exclaimed. This difference of opinion over the merits of our furry friends as home-sharers has permanently clouded a youthful relationship.

Our companion, I explain carefully to my son later, represents contemporary man, the spirit of animal rights and tolerance for all creatures great and small. Those of us who regard rabbits as an old-fashioned pest, to be shot on sight, are out of kilter with the mood of the times. Yet when I see as much as a rabbit dropping on my lawn, and the nibbled wreckage of a rose in the border, the urge for vengeance rises irresistibly in my throat. Yes, dear boy. Get the gun.

24

GOING NORTH

FOR A CENTURY and a half, for every sportsman the summer train to Scotland has possessed the thrill of a magic carpet. No artist has more vividly captured the sensation than George Earl, who in the early 1890s painted his huge canvases *Going North* and *Coming South*. Here are all the wealth, energy, confidence – and of course, passion for field sports – of high Victorian Britain.

At one time and another, I have stared fascinated at them for hours in this gallery and that. I have prints of them before me now. And as I gaze, I can summon up all the excitement of a summer evening at Euston, nursing the knowledge that by morning one will be trundling through the last glorious miles before Inverness.

Going North depicts King's Cross: the train at the platform proclaims its route as 'King's Cross & Aberdeen via Forth & Tay bridges'. And what's this shaft of strong morning sunlight piercing the smoky canopy of the station? Of course! It was no sleeper then, but a day train north with an overnight stop, which caused Trollope's Lady Eustace so much embarrassment over her diamonds.

Sprawling across the foreground of Earl's painting is an extraordinary galaxy of characters – I can count fifty-nine figures in all, along with twenty dogs. There are grandees and ghillies, footmen and young blades, lovers and porters and duchesses. The sense of expectation is captured best by the dogman kneeling among his setters. This is his first big test of the year. He knows his beauties will give of their best. The wide eyes of the small boy beside him reflect his excitement. Will this be his first experience of the champagne of the hills? On the right a young hero is trying to persuade a hesitant-looking girl that the pointer pups are simply marvellous, darling, and it would be no trouble to have one at home in Ebury Street. Fat chance.

The gun case marked 'Baggage Bombay' must belong to an imperial servant who has been dreaming of home leave through three years roasting in Bangalore – he could be part of the family whose ayah is reassuring the child looking so nervously at the artist. That long gaff and non-retractable net seem clumsy things to lug along a river-bank. But then, there's sure to be a ghillie to carry them.

I wouldn't much care to draw as a lodge companion the woman with the toy dog which looks like her lunch. She would be a fiend at bridge and lay down the law something shocking about the folly of letting Winifred marry a sugar broker. Oh God – I see a bundle of golf clubs. There has to be a troublemaker in every party.

The dog van lined with straw awaits the marvellous canine legion. In those days plenty of setters and pointers lived in the south for most of the year and the partridges. The clergyman studying his Bradshaw looks severe, but he is probably going north only to study John Knox. And among the sportsmen and their spouses weaves the shifting cast of servants and attendants: footmen carrying m'lady's rug and magazines, porters and a platform bookseller, valets and keepers. They know that they all have a part to play in the first act of one of the greatest of all British sporting pageants.

At Perth Station in *Coming South*, the clock shows ten to four. Everybody seems to be wearing immense quantities of clothes for September. Ah, much more likely it is October. In those leisured days, few gentlemen would think of coming home till the leaves were falling. I count eighty-four figures and fifteen dogs here. I am still pondering whether the brown-clad dog handler in the painting is the figure whom we saw earlier at King's Cross, having grown his whiskers for a couple of months. But no – the dogs are different.

A keeper touches his forelock to a gun, bidding farewell to the dogs which have served him so well. Somebody's got his flask up now the master in ensconced in his carriage – probably one of those ghillies whom fishers were instructed not to allow more than one soda-water bottle of whisky a day. The pointer sniffing the stray grouse feather on the platform is perfect, as is the woman beside him, clutching the white parasol. She makes it plain that whatever the social charms of the Highlands, she never much cared for those smelly brutes in the kennels. 'Nor did we, madam,' echoes that snooty footman carrying her fur wrap. Madam has dropped her book but she's damned if she will pick it up herself. What are servants for?

An elderly, tartan-clad figure is taking an emotional farewell of his granddaughter. Going south to be a lady's maid? The mustachioed spiv in brown disdains the proffered *Scotsman* – prefers his pink'un, no doubt. As for all the beards – heaven knows how those men got kissed at all. One of the facial funguses appears to be clasping the arm of the girl at whom he is looking adoringly – no, it's his cigar. Cavalier fellow; he can perfectly well see the No Smoking sign.

The dogs, the game – grouse, a hare, see the blackcock down there? – are the stars of this production. I'm sorry to see no salmon basses, but they are already stowed in the van. The two men chatting back there, one of them with a rod, probably haven't met since their ways parted towards the Tay and the Spey weeks ago. We know this much – they have done better than we shall this year.

The footman in his magnificent topper does not look enthusiastic about the setters in his charge: probably a cockney deeply grateful that his summer in the north, being ragged and condescended to in the kitchen by a lot of uncouth kilts, is over at last. He is returning to his natural habitat in a basement below Eaton Square. He is thinking: 'Please gawd that bloody keeper is at King's Cross to take the dogs off to Hampshire where they belong.'

It's time to go. The old train will puff its way southwards, chuntering faster and faster as it leaves the hills behind, blowing ashes through the window of any compartment brave enough to keep its window open. The rest of us are left to gaze upon the empty platform of Perth Station

– still recognizably the same vista those century-past sportsmen knew – to cherish and embroider in our own imagination the peerless story George Earl spun for posterity.

25

HEAVENLY GROUSE

AMONG SHOOTERS, 1997 and 1998 will be remembered as the Years of Hope. After a decade or more of relentless decline in Scottish grouse, some Angus and Perthshire moors again achieved 200-brace days. Euphoria reigned in parts of Scotland where despair had been endemic. Pessimists, who had doubted whether Scottish grouse would ever come back, were triumphantly routed. Yorkshire and Lancashire had their disappointments. But no one seriously doubts the long-term staying power of the great English moors, while the whole future of grouse shooting in Scotland has been hanging in the balance.

Beyond the familiar story of the grouse cycle, the message from most moors, above all those in Scotland, seems clear: if an owner is prepared to spend money upon intensive keepering on a scale unthought of a decade ago – though familiar to every landowner before the war – remarkable things are possible. It is now almost universally accepted that in the past Highland estates in particular were not nearly energetic enough in their approach to deer, sheep, stoats, rabbits and foxes. No sporting shooter doubts the seriousness of the raptor problem. But most people are also prepared to acknowledge that raptors are not the only issue – they have been allowed to become an all-purpose excuse for some moors.

The demand for driven-grouse shooting has never been greater. Many moors belong to rich men who let little or none of their shooting. As a result, those who take tenants can charge the earth: £80 or £90 a brace is average, and some Scottish moors have been extracting over £100 from big southern letting agencies (who obviously pile on their own percentage). Even at this grotesque level, they find takers.

Here is partly our old friend corporate hospitality at work. For a company, these costs are meaningless. But the consequences are pretty sore for private tenants paying out of their own pockets. Corporate clients drive up the cost of employing lawyers to insane heights, because companies involved in big suits scarcely glance at their legal bills. Companies establish the norms which private clients somehow have to go along with. Much the same is now true in the shooting field.

I go weak at the knees at the possibility of a day in the butts. The excitement of meeting those peerless birds exploding over the horizon from all angles and at all speeds is unmatched. For a start, with driven grouse you always know that if you do the business right yourself, almost every bird is within range. The variety of shots is astonishing. Although I am resigned to my own erratic marksmanship, against driven grouse my performance fluctuates dramatically even by the usual standard. At some drives, birds are coming straight forward, over one's head. However fast, I can usually make a reasonable show at these. But more often, they are crossing in front. One is snatching a shot before they head for somebody else. Those diagonal birds I miss in coveys. Things get worse if my neighbour happens to be one of those serious grouse shooters who do little else between August and December. The more lethally I see the next butt perform, the more jumpy and ineffective I myself become. Each drive I promise that I shall wipe the slate clean and do better, only to find suddenly that five butts have come and gone and it is time to go home, nursing one's memories and frustrations. I kid myself that nowadays I am not a jealous man – I am hugely grateful for all the fun and sport I get. But show me a man who gets, say, ten or twelve days a year at driven grouse, and I go slowly green. It remains the most thrilling shooting sport in the world – which is why the richest men in the world converge on northern England and Scotland every year to spend a significant fraction of their fortunes pursuing it.

Happily, however, unless one is very lazy it is not necessary to sit in a butt to shoot grouse. I never say no to walking in line, because any chance to go to the hill is worth selling one's soul for. I regret only that walking-up is unsociable. Nobody minds the puffing and panting – indeed I love it – but in line, one can't have the jolly running gossip with neighbours which is part of the joy of all field sports. I am also jaundiced, because in line I am pathetically prone to be caught wrong-footed when the birds get up.

Dogging still makes my heart leap, as it did when first I tried it thirty years ago. The beauty of the animals; the joy of watching the Highland dance of dogs, handlers, grouse and guns; the pleasure of being able to walk in company until there is a point; all combine to create a perfect sporting occasion. I started dogging on a little moor in Sutherland, which I first rented in 1971 when it cost us £500 to shoot 100 brace of grouse over a couple of weeks. In more recent years, I have enjoyed seeing Angus Ross, the Achentoul keeper, work his brilliant pointers across the hills at the head of the strath.

Almost every grouse season, a four-by-four towing a small trailer trundles off the Irish ferry, bringing Billy Hosick and his dogs – twenty-three of them, to be precise – on a pilgrimage to Inverness-shire. I have been privileged to be a spectator of Hosick's operations for a number of years, and I doff my cap to this supreme sportsman. He is now sixty-seven, a retired garage owner from just outside Belfast, who takes to the hills with his leads, shorts and inimitable Northern Irish accent to give a perfect demonstration of how dogs should work a grouse moor. Most of his animals are setters. Perhaps it is only when one has seen really bad dogs work a hill – bursting into every covey, running miles out of sight, missing half the ground – that one appreciates just how good Hosick's setters are.

They are beautiful on their leashes in his hand, and they become a hundred times more so as they race across the heather, quartering the hill in front of the guns with perfect symmetry then freezing for that heart-stopping moment, which means that it is time for the guns to load and hasten. There is nothing to beat those last moments of tension before the birds explode from the heather, as the guns search uncertainly to guess where they lie, to discuss whether there is an old cock, a barren pair or a big covey crouching within shot. This is true sport, hunting sport, and it would be impossible without the great corps of dog-handling wizards like Hosick.

So much is alleged about cruelties among trainers that it is striking to see his gentleness with his dogs, even when they err. 'I hardly ever sell a grown dog, Max,' he said. 'I can't bear to see them go, because so few people have any idea about how to treat them.' He is right. Pointers and setters need the sort of exercise and supervision that scarcely any amateur possesses the space and skill to provide. Billy spends most of his hours with his dogs and they repay him a hundredfold. Having won almost every prize, he has virtually given up competing. He simply loves to run his dogs on the hill for the pleasure they give him and the rest of us. He and his brand of sport are the kind which give grouse shooting a good name. I cherish the memory of his bronze-coated beauties dancing through the heather and frozen on point beside the guns. I hope fervently to see them do the same next year. Pheasants is optional, I say, but grouse is compulsory.

26

DRIVEN OFF THE TEE

I AM ALLERGIC TO golf and cats. Ten pennyworth of lead can deal with the latter. Golf, on the other hand, is always with us, along with its dreadful clothing, customs, jokes, enthusiasts and snobbery. A friend of mine who, in a rash moment, built a course on his own estate, described the other day how he was playing a round with a friend, when a foursome in front picked a fight. One of them, indeed, roundly abused him. 'I hate to mention it, but I do happen to own this course,' said my friend mildly. 'I couldn't give a ****,' said his adversary with contempt.

You see what I mean? If you play golf, never mind own a golf club, you are liable to meet people who seem to have escaped from a Florida TV soap. Prince Andrew – *Prince Andrew* – has become the game's royal patron in Britain. The only white man I ever heard of on a golf course was dear old Bill Deedes.

By now you may be asking: 'What has happened to Hastings lately, to cause him to work himself into such a fever about this harmless and engaging game?' Nothing, absolutely nothing, I assure you. Well, that is, unless you include a trifling episode a few months ago on the Berkshire Downs. My teenage son and a visiting friend were silly enough to say they'd like to play a round. I pick up a golf club about once every four years, almost always to stroll around an undistinguished but pretty course on the edge of the Thames escarpment, to keep friends company. It was thither that we drove on a sunny summer morning. The boys had a set of clubs. On arrival we hired another, bought a few balls and lobbed out £70 – yes, good grief, I would have thought you could play at Augusta for less – in green fees. But I suppose I should have realized that times had changed, and pretensions grown at that little course, as soon as I saw the old wooden clubhouse was gone, and been replaced by a squat structure in brick and plate glass, heavily adorned with notices about Correct Behaviour.

Our performance at the first tee was undistinguished, shall we say. We giggled a bit about what idiots we must have looked to onlookers and prepared to set off after the balls, an undemanding distance down the fairway. At that moment, however, from the clubhouse emerged a large figure, lumbering majestically towards us in a manner that recalled the old village policeman preparing to deal with a small boy found bicycling without lights, or my late housemaster on discovering Molesworth minor lighting up behind the squash court.

'Are any of you people *golfers?*' he enquired. It just shows how spoilt some of us get in middle age, that I had to reverse my mind thirty years to remember being addressed with such scorn. 'I mean, do any of you belong to any club? Do you have handicaps? How do you propose to play golf without a set of clubs for each of you?'

And so on and so on. I mumbled explanations about keeping the boys company, about having pottered round the course occasionally for years, about managing perfectly well, thank you. Our clothes didn't find much favour either, it seemed. My son was wearing a shirt without a collar. We hadn't a golf shoe between us. Humiliation heaped upon humiliation.

Well, the long and the short of it was that I slunk back to the pro shop and was handed my money, in return for removing our presence from the hallowed turf. It's years since I was run out of somewhere. I'd forgotten how it felt. There were all those men watching from the clubhouse, impeccably dressed in their tartan slacks, co-respondent shoes and baseball caps. I felt like the victim of a Bateman joke: 'THE MAN WHO THOUGHT HE COULD TURN OUT ON A GOLF COURSE WITHOUT A BOBBLE CAP, CHECKED TROUSERS AND A STRIPED UMBRELLA.'

As we drove home, nursing our shame, I asked myself if I could imagine shooters or fishers behaving in a similar fashion. What would any of us do if somebody turned up on the river-bank in denims instead of breeches, or arrived to shoot clutching a muzzle-loader and wearing an old blue overcoat? Welcome him in, from my experience. Surely only the most pompous grandees get in a state about dress or, for that matter, about incompetence unless one is actively dangerous.

I submit that one of the problems about golf is that a good many of the people who play (or, more important, who hang around the clubhouse) want to make a social statement. Hence all those frightful public rows about suburban golf courses which even these days try to exclude women, other races or people who don't turn up at Rotary. Since my own little rebuff, I have been offered many words of wisdom from golfing acquaintances. 'The litmus test,' announced one sage, 'is whether they'll let you bring your dog on the course. If they do, it is a gentleman's establishment. If they don't, it's for upwardly mobile plasterers and decorators.'

Everybody has his own horror story about being evicted from the clubhouse bar for wearing the wrong shoes or for failing to make indecent advances to the president's wife. The vital thing, so I am told, is never to make jokes about golf. You may tell dirty stories if you like. But you must understand that The Game is a matter of deadly earnest, unfit for mockery by the sort of people who play it.

So there you are. That day on the Berkshire Downs explains how my distaste for golf has escalated into passionate loathing, a yearning to drive my Land Rover across the very next green I see, preferably in the midst of a championship. I shall now, however, spoil my case by telling a story about my own golfing history which offers a hole-in-one to the club secretary who threw us out. Twenty years ago in Ireland, keeping a friend company on a Kilkenny course, we had been waiting an eternity on the tee for a foursome on the green.

'Oh, for God's sake, Max, get on with it,' said my friend. 'You're not going to get anywhere near them.' I then hit the only perfect golf shot of my life. The ball lifted, soared, flew straight as a die down the course. We began to think it would get somewhere near the green. Belatedly, we cried,

'Fore!' One of that foursome lifted his head in response. My ball smote him full toss in the midst of the temple. He dropped like a stone.

I was terrified. I assumed I had committed manslaughter on the links. But when the man woke up, a good minute later, amid his dazed stupor he announced calmly, 'Don't worry about a thing. Anybody could have done it. Think no more about it,' and staggered off to his car. It is unjust to suggest that Bill Deedes is golf's only white man. That doughty citizen of Kilkenny in the 1970s remains my hero. Yet the nineties being what they are, I have a horrible feeling that if I did the same again today, he'd sue.

27

To the Manor Born

On 4 november 1897, Lord Ashburton and a team of six other semi-professional assassins killed 1,461 partridges in a single day at The Grange in Hampshire. At least two and possibly three teams of beaters marshalled the menu for this great occasion, directed by the head keeper galloping about on a sturdy grey horse. Those were the days when pheasants and hares were treated as near-vermin on those great chalk-land manors. The long stubbles left by the binder provided perfect habitat for the English partridge, agreed by one and all to be the perfect gentleman among gamebirds.

The Grange's performance was outdone by Holkham, where they shot 1,671 partridges in twenty drives on a single day in 1905. The Duke of Portland shot 1,478 in a day at Welbeck in 1906, but no doubt Lord Ashburton consoled himself with the knowledge that, over three days, he achieved an unsurpassed 3,536, God help us. At The Grange a decade earlier, Lord Walsingham was one of a team of seven who shot 4,109 over a week. 'No red legs, all grey birds, one very weak gun in the team,' he wrote irritably. 'Fifteen to eighteen short drives each day. I got 340 the first day, my best drives 42, 62, 74. Another good gun would have made a difference of 600 in the week.'

The numbers sound grotesque to our modern ear. But anyone today who has caught a glimpse of living sporting history, by seeing coveys of wild partridges exploding over the hedges, wings set, feels privileged. There are now only a handful of places, most of them in East Anglia, where by heroic exertions people like Hugh van Cutsem at Hilborough manage to produce showy bags of wild English partridges. It would be optimistic to imagine that, even with more sensitive farming practice, they will be brought back on a scale to justify shooting huge numbers, even if anyone was crass enough to want to.

Most people who shoot partridges in Britain today, and for the foreseeable future, depend upon reared birds, the majority Frenchmen. But over the past decade or two, on many shoots there has been a great improvement in their management. There was a time when being invited to shoot tame partridges was almost as embarrassing as a date to pot reared ducks. In many places, they were reluctant to fly at all. When they were shuffled into the air, birds would flutter unwillingly forward, before dropping down in front of the guns for a bracing walk home. Some partridge drives resembled November grouse days in one sense only – half the birds disappeared out of the sides, never to be seen again, while the rest poured over the line in a great pack which provoked a thirty-second Somme barrage followed by a morning's silence.

But today that sort of thing seems a bad memory. Keepers have mastered the art of rearing and showing partridges, anywhere the terrain gives them a sporting chance to do so. The rewards are tremendous for shooters, who get the chance of some seriously exciting October or November days, at a time when, if pheasants fly at all, they look pretty miserable about it.

Gerald Boord now farms Northington, part of the old Grange estate where Lord Ashburton made his huge bags. For many years in modern times Northington has been chiefly a massed low-pheasant shoot – they killed over 10,000 in 1982. But when Gerald took it over eleven years ago, he made up his mind to concentrate on quality partridges once more. Today he has made a notable success of this. His keeper Peter Bushell rears some 5,000 French and 1,000 English. They aim to shoot 250 or so a day, about 28 days a year, over some of their 1,700 acres. In 1996, they killed 3,092 French, 315 grey partridges and 2,093 pheasants.

What makes the shoot are the hedges – the best sort of thick, high Hampshire field boundaries which force the birds to soar upwards to clear them, and present some marvellous shooting to guns lining out 20 yards behind. Gerald makes everybody stand dead on the pegs – no shirkers sneaking back 10 yards to give themselves more time to get the gun up. The name of the game is snap shooting, and what enormous fun it is.

The point of standing up close is to make the sport hard and fast, to meet the birds before they drop down again, and to improve the quarry's chances a little. Let us be honest – in some respect partridges are forgiving. Unless there's a gale blowing, they fly more slowly than grouse or pheasants, and it takes significantly less lead to bring them down. Again and again, we've all dropped partridges with a couple of pellets, when the same shot would scarcely slow a pheasant. Gerald Boord has one stand he is justly proud of, only a couple of hundred yards from his own house. The birds are driven out of a game crop. Most of them have to climb a cluster of ash trees to reach the guns. By the time they get to the line, they are marvellously high and fast. The thrill of snatching for those dashing little birds almost matches that of grouse.

In all the excitement, I started making the mistakes one always does when one hurries too much: closing the gun on only a single cartridge (and then of course wasting it); changing one's mind about which bird to shoot; firing underneath the away bird behind. The shade of old Lord Ashburton would treat some of the Boord team with respect – the West Country contingent were chillingly deadly. At one drive the wind was blowing birds along the line, and scarcely anything survived the Devon mafiosi to get as far as me. When the wind and the numbering was reversed, I explained that it was my natural sense of sporting generosity which spared huge packs to float their way.

The beating was exemplary, with the line halting at every flush, so that the birds came forward in a steady stream through the drives. Like every other sort of shooting, partridge days profit hugely from a wind, and we were lucky to have a steady breeze all morning. Even the best shoots can look a bit sad on still days early in the season. Gerald arranged our day on 4 November 1997, the centenary of the Ashburton orgy. Nobody was trying to break any records. The shooting by the serious players was so straight in the morning that the beaters speeded up the drives after lunch, to keep the bag within sensible limits. We ended up with 179 brace of partridges and 68 pheasants, which the old lord a hundred years ago would scarcely have deemed worth getting out of bed for, but which all of us enjoyed hugely.

That splendid sporting artist Rodger McPhail was one of the team, and he has painted a picture to celebrate the occasion. I think we all thought of it as a celebration of partridge shooting as much as an outing at Northington. The pattern of shooting has changed immeasurably over the past one hundred years. Few of us will ever know the glories of shooting coveys of wild English partridges in stubbles. But the best of the modern sport provides a splendid substitute. A high-flying reared partridge over a Hampshire hedge possesses a grace and charm that makes a good many pheasants look commonplace by comparison.

28

TREE MADNESS

THE OTHER DAY I found myself at the same table as a timber merchant. Not surprisingly, we began to talk about trees. 'Of course, nothing grown in this country is any use for construction,' he said cheerfully. 'It's all just pulp and chipboard, pulp and chipboard.' Yes, we've heard all that before. But a spontaneous surge of rage shot through me as I summoned up a vision of all the upland horizons in this overcrowded island, devastated by reckless softwood planting over the past sixty or seventy years. I fish most seasons on the Naver, whose upper reaches are marred by

some horrible post-war planting, today uneconomic to thin
or extract. Much of the great county of Sutherland, come
to that, is defaced by conifer forests which have inflicted
deadly damage upon sport for no lasting benefit to employment, and created a great green blight across the beauty of
so many hillsides.

Mounting, if not irrefutable, evidence emphasizes the
damage conifers do to salmon rivers through acidification
as well as hill drainage. A passionate fan of John Buchan,
I weep for the great tracts of south-west Scotland, his
stamping grounds of Dumfries and Galloway, buried for
ever beneath miles of wretched trees. In the far north some
greedy landowners have lately been able to enrich themselves by accepting government subsidies *not* to plant
conifers. But far more have seized the cash benefits of
putting in miles of pine and spruce. Huge areas of the
uplands of Scotland, Wales and England are today covered
in softwood, which could possess no possible economic
justification had it not been planted and maintained with
taxpayers' money. And still, in some areas, even after steep
reductions in tax relief, the folly goes on.

Most of us would divide disasters into two kinds –
avoidable and unavoidable. Floods, earthquakes and my
difficulties hitting high pheasants might be described as
the hand of fate. But ever since large-scale softwood planting
began in Britain, a host of prophets have denounced its
follies and warned of its consequences. In the early 1970s I
made a film for the BBC about the conifer madness. The
advocates of planting trotted out all the familiar arguments:
'pit props for trenches in the next war', 'import saving',
'improving empty landscape'. And do you know, some
people actually believed this guff. The Forestry Commission
had the neck to suggest that it was 'creating a tourist
amenity' by planting thousands of acres of wonderful open

moorland with conifers, and then sticking 'picnic areas' in the middle of them.

It was forcefully argued by sensible people that if a fraction of the subsidy given to trees was diverted to hill farmers, the long-term benefits to employment would be far greater. But no one in office took any notice. An unholy alliance of powerful upland landowners and Scottish trades unionists mounted one of the most successful lobbies of modern times to induce government to encourage softwood planting, by pouring tens of millions of grants and tax reliefs into it. I remember one of these lunatics (the land-owners, that is) solemnly assuring me that his group wanted to see no more than 17 per cent of Scotland under conifers. Why 17 per cent, rather than 23 per cent or 6 per cent or 80 per cent, God knows (in the same way that only He knows why one of those characters in Broadmoor thinks he is Napoleon rather than Hitler, Charlie Chaplin or William Hague). But no doubt the foresters saw a logic in all this at the time.

It is baffling that government did not. As early as 1972, a Treasury review of forestry was fiercely critical of the economic performance of British forestry. An independent National Audit Office report in 1986 was even more savage. 'On any sensible assumptions,' said the NAO, 'forestry represents a highly expensive mechanism for job creation. Agriculture and other forms of development are significantly less costly, and provide employment in the near and medium rather than the distant future.'

Nigel Lawson as Chancellor acted to remove many of the tax concessions for forestry in his 1988 Budget, but still planting continues, not least because those with big investments in forestry cannot bring themselves to acknowledge that this is not an economic proposition, any more than it is an environmentally sane one. Today 3½ million acres of Britain are under forestry, one-seventh of this total being broadleaf trees, virtually all the latter in England. Scottish planting is almost entirely coniferous, and unlikely ever to make sense even to those who have invested fortunes in it. Worst of all, land that has been planted is lost for ever to the heather, because even when it has been clear-felled, it is unsuitable for further use. It becomes a barren wilderness.

Those landowners who have planted trees in Scotland have deluded both themselves about the figures, and their posterity about the destruction of the landscape and its sporting potential. Only foxes and other predators flourish in pine plantations, with disastrous consequences for other kinds of wildlife. It remains a mystery how some 'forestry advisers' successfully convinced ministers and landowners that good trees would ever flourish amid the gales endemic in many parts of the Highlands.

I am not talking here about sensible shelter belts, but about mile upon mile of stunted Christmas trees. What of those lairds who abandoned hope of their grouse in the 1970s and 1980s and put their moors under trees? Today, some of them bitterly regret it. But it is too late. They have permanently destroyed a whole environment by short-sighted deployment of what Evelyn Waugh memorably described as 'that sly instinct for self-preservation which passes for wisdom among the rich'. Michael Wigan, himself a Highland landowner, has written with splendid tren-chancy and penetration about the folly of so much Scottish tree-planting. Yet still many of those involved, up to and including government and the Highland development bodies, will not admit the truth.

By the time some of the forestry lobby have read this far, they will already be penning letters lamenting 'Max Hastings's irrational hatred of trees' as they have done whenever I have written this sort of piece at intervals for almost thirty years. I withdraw nothing. Of course I support hardwood planting, and softwood planting for amenity or shelter purposes. There are areas of Britain which are neither suitable for agriculture, nor possess any scenic beauty, where forestry should be welcomed – tracts of the Midlands spring to mind.

But those who continue to press for yet more wholesale afforestation in our uplands should be prepared to answer the following questions: could domestic softwood planting in Britain ever justify the environmental damage it does by generating significant levels of lasting employment? Could conifers ever produce profit as a simple commercial investment, without assistance of one kind or another from the taxpayer? Could conifers ever produce import savings of sufficient benefit to the British economy, to compensate for the destruction of our priceless uplands?

I believe that the answer to all these question is no. I suggest that, in the long term, afforestation and inshore salmon farms will prove to have been two disastrous environmental delusions for our great wildernesses. Our children and grandchildren will think we were mad ever to have fallen for the claptrap of the forestry lobby and its tax advisers. And when we are working to defend the record of private landowners as stewards of our countryside, the blot on the record which will be hardest to erase is that created by those who took the forestry pieces of silver for a mess of pottage, to mix metaphors.

So there. I feel better having vented my spleen. But I would feel better still if I could take a few picnics in the upland woods with a can of petrol and a box of matches.

29

GUNS AND SHOOTERS

IT WOULD SEEM paradoxical to many townspeople that though I shoot, like most shooters, I do not think of myself a gun enthusiast. A few people indeed build up armouries of weapons because they love them; some regard them as works of art. Rather more are like me, and own guns simply as tools with which to practise a sport. If we gave up shooting, we would sell the guns or hand them on to our children.

My father was different. He was a passionate if erratic collector, and the house was always littered with a miscellany of antique firearms, some of which he prized highly enough to like to see around him daily, on his desk or on his library shelves. As a child, they fascinated me. There was a beautiful .44 Navy Colt. I never fired lead through it, but often set percussion caps on the nipples of its cylinder and fanned the hammer in approved Western manner, to produce a gratifying haze of smoke. The .44 was a single-action model, which I admired more than its repeating counterpart on the window sill, a clumsy early version from around 1870.

For many years the pride of Father's collection was a pair of early-nineteenth-century percussion duelling pistols. I was taught to admire their perfect balance and engraving, the meticulous accessories in the baize-lined case. I was also told never to press the trigger and release the hammer. One day I forgot, causing both the hammer and Father's temper to shear. The pair eventually disappeared from the house, bound for a saleroom, during one of his recurrent financial crises. In contradiction of what I wrote above, if I had inherited those minor works of art, I would have kept them, though I would not spend my own money to buy their like.

Father could not stop himself acquiring weapons of neither use nor beauty, merely because of his inability to venture anywhere near a gun sale without attaching himself to something. There was a pair of late-nineteenth-century Austrian Steyr rifles, which he was quite unable to explain to me (far less to my stepmother) why he had brought home one day. He never fired them, and they languished in the attic until they were resold. There were also lots of shotguns. He was a personal friend of Robert Churchill the gunmaker, and any visit to the shop was liable to result in further damage to his overdraft. I can seldom remember him raising a gun to wildfowl, but he owned a three-inch chambered 12-bore of Churchill's as well as the inevitable pair of game guns and a wide variety of other stuff picked up over the years.

Shortly before he died, he inflicted on me a curious, almost biblical trial by ordeal. He told me suddenly: 'I don't want to see the Churchills any more. Take the pair away and do what you want with them.' Forty-eight hours later, he telephoned me in a rage: 'What have you done with my guns? How dare you take them. Bring them back at once.' The pain of parting had proved too great. He had changed his mind. I was very hurt, of course, but I understood. He kept the guns until he died. When I inherited them, to my sadness, I found myself obliged to take them to the saleroom. He shot off the left shoulder, and the stocks were too heavily cast as well as much too short for me, a right-hander. I preserved, as an act of filial piety, only his cherished muzzle-loading shotguns, one flintlock and two percussion, though I have never carried devotion so far as to use them on game as he did. I have quite enough trouble connecting with a bird when I am armed with a modern weapon, never mind attacking pheasants wreathed in black powder smoke and trembling about the risk of a barrel burst. Pierce Egan observed 150 years ago: 'Gentlemen cannot too often be warned that, while they increase, by the use of the double-barrelled fowling piece, their chance of execution only two-fold, they may at the same time increase perhaps a hundred-fold, the chance of injuring themselves.'

Like many boys of my time, I started shooting with a rather nasty Belgian folding .410, before graduating to a Wilkes 20-bore which I grew very fond of. My own sixteen-year-old is now snooty about 20-bores and keeps asking when he can use a 12. But as I bought a nice pair of Spanish 20-bore sidelocks for my children a few years ago, I tell him he should think himself lucky. When I was eighteen, my father gave me a Webley & Scott boxlock 12-bore which I cherish to this day as a rough-shooting gun. It cost £120, which seemed a substantial sum of money thirty-five years ago. But it has done me a lot of service, and remains ideal for those days when one is more likely than not to fall into something wet, horrible and probably rocky.

I have used for many years a Brno .22, which I bought myself for about £40 when I was twenty-one. I know that a lot of serious vermin shooters consider a semi-automatic rifle essential, but I don't think I have missed many bunnies because of the bolt-action. The Brno is a trifle rusty and battered now but shoots as straight as I do, which is all one can ask of any gun. I keep a sixty-year-old Browning pump-action .22 of Father's only because my son begs me to. However often I suggest that it is a much less accurate and reliable tool than the Brno, he points out that he loves firing it, so I succumb. I felt the same at his age.

When I sold Father's Churchills, I bought myself a good Watson sidelock which served me well for some years. Then it suffered a nasty muzzle-burst – I suspect because I had been careless enough to let mud get in – and I had to have it rebarrelled, very expensively since I found that my insurance didn't cover the damage. Illogically, I never felt quite the same about it after that and, when one day I kidded myself that I had some money, I sold it and bought a pair of Atkins, with which I shoot to this day. Every now and again I tell myself that I am not a rich enough man to have so much money tied up in shotguns. I also wonder how long one will have a chance regularly to shoot with two guns in Britain. But then I consider the wonderful pleasure I gain from using those guns, and I know I shall stick with them for as long as I shoot.

They were built in the 1920s and bear the somewhat

cheeky inscription 'Henry Atkin from Purdeys', which I suspect no gunmaker would be allowed to get away with these days, under the Trades Description Act. It sounds a bit like me describing myself as 'Max Hastings, from the *Daily Telegraph*'. But the engraving, the actions and the stocks of those Atkins are superb. I know that if I do my stuff, so will those guns. Even though I admire and cherish them, I never give them a moment's thought between February and August each year. They stay locked up. I feel no urge to gaze at them or play with them as did my father or as I did as a teenager. I lack the instincts of a gun collector. For me they are simply the means to an end, not an end in themselves. It is the pageant of shooting which draws me out into the countryside on so many autumn and winter days, not the desire to handle a weapon. No, I have to tell the opponent of game shooting, it would not be at all the same if we were only permitted to march in threes to a licensed shooting ground on a frosty morning and fire at targets. For most of us the game is the thing, not the gun.

Yet sporting gun owners in many parts of the country report evidence that police hostility to them is growing. All sorts of people, including keepers and stalkers, have tales to tell of bureaucratic obstruction or even harassment, inspired simply by mounting pressures upon the fact of private gun ownership. A cynic might suggest that the police aspire to see a society in which the possession of firearms is confined to their own ranks and those of professional criminals.

In fairness to the police, it must be acknowledged that their attitude mirrors that of a wider public. Tony Blair's Government is keen to see the Army Cadet Force expand among teenagers – but is unkeen that they should be allowed to do weapon-training. Many people now look on guns as inherently disagreeable. They do not distinguish between types; they simply associate weapons with danger and evil. Where once guns were perceived as natural instruments of pleasure and honourable military purpose, today they are regarded as tools for terrorists and murderers. Many think the world can be made less dangerous, murderous and evil if there are fewer legally held guns in private hands, no matter what use these are put to. It was under a Tory Home Secretary, Michael Howard, that the first steps were taken to make shooters pariahs, by the banning of pistol ownership.

I sometimes point out that after the Second World War there were incomparably more guns in British homes than there are today. Scarcely a hall cupboard lacked its war souvenirs, which in my father's case included a couple of Lugers, a broom-handle Mauser, a Polish Radom – oh, yes, and a Schmeisser machine-pistol and lots of 9mm ammunition. When I was about eleven, I amused myself by stripping these toys on the kitchen table when there was nobody around to object.

At that period, despite the huge arsenal of deadly weapons in circulation, nothing remotely resembling the Hungerford or Dunblane nightmares took place. We were a different sort of country – and one in which most men were accustomed to firearms, whether by choice or necessity. They had spent years with a rifle or revolver as a daily companion, its presence taken for granted. Policemen were equally familiar with guns. Not perceived as good or bad, they were simply a fact of life.

Even the post-war generation routinely learnt to handle weapons. In the school cadet force and later in the Territorial Army, I shot with rifle, Bren, Browning and Sterling, often at Bisley whose charitable status has lately been questioned. As Charterhouse teenagers, like thousands of others, we cycled around the Surrey countryside with fully operational rifles or Stens slung over our shoulders. Nobody thought anything of it. Can you imagine what an uproar there would be if such a convoy was sighted on the public highway today?

We have moved into the era of hi-tech warfare. It seems likely that any future conflict involving British forces will be decided between rival forces of specialists, armed with electronically guided weaponry. The divide between civilian society and the shrinking private world of the armed forces has never been wider. The old world of the militia, the volunteers, who honed the skills of riflemen on a thousand weekend ranges up and down the country, has passed.

All those young heroes of G. A. Henty's novels, who were assured by Uncle that their futures were secure, provided they learnt to ride, swim, become a useful rifle shot and keep their clean limbs off women and drink, would be a mite baffled by the skills urged upon your ambitious young Brit of today: get a computer quick, don't snort cocaine in your own office and make sure any girl you get pregnant has signed a prenuptial. Gosh, not much there about the merits of holding your breath and squeezing the trigger rather than jerking it if you want to drop your Dervish at two hundred paces. Cadet forces no longer allow range practice at human-figure targets. I wonder whether Gerry Adams and his friends harmonize on these matters.

We must acknowledge that the value of teaching marksmanship to civilians for national defence has gone. But that seems no reason to declare that, since firearms are no longer a necessary evil, they deserve wholesale banishment. Although it is unfashionable to say so, the military skills one learnt as a teenager gave a lot of harmless help to the self-confidence of young things like me. I was hopeless on the school games field. To make up, I learnt to read a map and use a compass, to parachute, camp in the wilderness and, yes, use a variety of weapons. I don't believe acquiring those skills encouraged anyone I knew to become a homicidal maniac.

At school, I remember one fatal accident and one suicide in which corps weapons were involved. A modern coroner, police investigation and media pack might make a fuss about the irresponsibility of allowing teenagers access to firearms. Yet how many ways can the young find to injure themselves, or other people, without a gun in sight?

The new hostility to guns has made most of us paranoid about their custody. We know how unforgiving the police can be if they are lost or stolen. When I stop for lunch on the way to Scotland I am petrified about securing the guns in the car. Yet when did one last hear of a crime committed with a stalking rifle? And how often does an armed criminal need recourse to a stolen Holland?

Those of us with access to a public platform must never tire of reminding the public – and policemen – of the legitimacy of sporting shooting, and of the negligible risks it poses to public safety. An unholy alliance of politicians and the media threatens the doctrine of proportionality. Proportionality – or rather, sanity – demands that the degree of restriction placed upon personal liberty should roughly correspond to the degree of risk posed by a given threat. For instance, some of us campaign against the fanatical lobbies pressing for ever more draconian drink-driving laws, because it is simply not true that this country has a serious drink-driving problem. Our roads are among the safest in the world.

Likewise on firearms: hundreds of thousands of people enjoy sporting shooting through the year, with perfect respect for the law and safety. Dunblane and Hungerford were appalling incidents, but they were representative of nothing – certainly not of any general threat to our society posed by legally held firearms. After Dunblane, I incurred the wrath of some shooters by saying publicly that there did seem a case for tighter controls on the private custody of large-calibre pistols. A certain kind of fantasist is specially attracted to playing with handguns. It seems reasonable that the law should draw a distinction between its treatment of guns designed for target and sporting use, and those which are manufactured for the explicit purpose of killing people. In the times in which we live, it seems fair to scrutinize closely the sort of person who feels he wants to use a Colt or Smith and Wesson magnum as a weekend toy.

But all that said, in 1996 when I supported a review of the private custody of full-bore pistols, it never crossed my mind that a hysterical body politic would proceed to ban the use of all pistols, even by Olympic competitors. This was an appalling breakdown of proportionality.

There is today a danger that the same philosophy will be extended to all firearms. There could be a steady growth of new restrictions, designed 'to prevent another Dunblane'. A senior minister told me recently that there are no *current* plans for changes in firearms legislation. But he added ominously, 'that is, unless someone does something terrible with a shotgun'. New measures could have a drastic impact on country sports. But they could never 'prevent another Dunblane'. Madmen will always find means to do terrible things, with or without the assistance of a police force, which at Dunblane blatantly failed to enforce existing law and has been trying to shift blame for its tragic lapse ever since.

Circumstances have combined to render the public increasingly intolerant of guns in private hands. In the nineteenth century, and even for much of the twentieth, the landowning classes possessed great economic and political power. Field sports were their amusements and, however much the intellectuals mocked, there was little political will to interfere. Today, power has shifted into the hands of the urban and suburban middle class. The media represent guns either as the tools of mass murderers or as weapons for the destruction of wild creatures, about which the public is intensely sentimental. The countryside is infinitely more crowded. Only in remote corners of Britain can a gun be let off without somebody hearing.

The police simply do not want the responsibility of monitoring private gun owners, or of taking the blame if their judgement proves wanting about who is and is not fit to own a gun. My own collection, rational enough to anyone who knows shooting, sounds an alarming armoury to anyone who does not. Many townspeople today are uneasy about the very notion of guns being held in private hands.

We need to be conscious of these attitudes in order to make the case for shooting. It is pointless for sporting magazines merely to offer ringing calls of defiance to their readers, shooters all. It is the non-shooting public whom we need to address and to reassure. In the next century, sporting shooters in Britain will keep guns only on the most delicate licence from the rest of society. It is sobering to consider that the political future is heavily dependent upon the behaviour of two forces entirely beyond our control: criminals and madmen.

30

HIGH PHEASANTS

MOST OF US would agree that for any activity to deserve to be called a sport, it should involve skill, chance and exertion. In shooting, the latter point makes some of us keen on rough days, when one has to walk for one's birds, rather than being driven from peg to peg at a covert shoot. Even rough-shooting one is sometimes presented with a pretty easy away shot at a bird flushed by one's feet. But more often walked-up birds of any kind take us by surprise. We miss plenty in consequence. Likewise, except at the start of the season, driven grouse are almost always challenging targets.

Driven pheasants are another cup of tea. In some measure, and in some parts of the country, modern sportsmen can be given a choice about how difficult they want the birds to be. The Edwardians demanded vast numbers to shoot at and didn't much care how high or low they were. Some modern tycoons, even experienced shots, seem perfectly happy to spend their shooting days mowing down huge numbers of easy chickens.

Most of us, however, even if we are not very proficient, like to be challenged. It has become a matter of endless debate and controversy just how difficult a 'good' pheasant should be. In some parts of the country, such as the Midlands, the terrain is so unhelpful that pheasants simply won't fly well unless a gale gives a helping hand. But a growing number of keen shots now focus their passions upon a handful of estates up and down Britain, where pheasants are driven over guns pushed to the limits of their sporting capabilities. Shooters speak with bated breath of Castle Hill or Haddeo Valley in Devon, Garrowby, Helmsley and Kepwick in Yorkshire, and some of the Welsh and Scottish border shoots.

What these places have in common is the right sort of ground. They possess steep escarpments off which birds can be driven. Sure, there are some miraculous shoots in East Anglia where pheasants come high and fast over the guns, even when pushed out of a game crop on billiard-table countryside. But for the most part, it is hill country which provides the most testing shooting in Britain. Critics declare that the very high shoots are artificial, because they are organized to show pheasants in a way that flouts natural behaviour. The birds are merely gliding fast downhill from an elevated launching pad. In varying degrees, all driven shooting is artificial. But I question whether the high shooting business is sporting when, first, a competent shot using a standard game gun and ammunition cannot achieve a respectable ratio of birds to cartridges. Sportsmen must always treat a living quarry with respect. Of course all of us sometimes, or even frequently, fail to kill what we shoot at. But there should be a reasonable expectation that success is achievable, when we raise the gun. I admire shoots such as Dumbleton in Gloucestershire or Conholt in Hampshire because while their birds are high, it is never in doubt that they are hittable. At Haddeo Valley in Devon, the splendid shoot chieftain Ned Goschen sometimes stands behind with a .410, potting birds the line have missed, to show that even a boy's gun can get the results in the right hands. That is not always true in Devon where one sees so many birds flinch in the air, then fly on. At some high-bird commercial shoots, also, the numbers reared are so grotesque that disease problems are inescapable. There are even reports of some shoots which pursue shameful late-release policies. This is deeply damaging to the reputation of shooting.

Yet, at its best, it is a marvellous experience to have the opportunity to shoot at high pheasants. The first challenge, for those of us who don't do it a lot, is to convince ourselves that we can do it at all. At Dumbleton, again and again, I have seen pheasants approach the line that I would not think worth a cartridge from my own gun, but which my host Charlie Hambro kills stone dead with awesome consistency. Once, when I was feeling especially inadequate next to my host, my loader said, 'You watch his lordship. You'll see that he always takes the same bird.' I could see what he meant. With casual elegance, Charlie has for years been shooting a bird which, however high, he knows exactly where to put the gun to bring down. You still need to be a very good shot to maintain that consistency of gun-mounting and swing. Those of us with more erratic habits are suitably jealous. We all cherish moments when we have shot a seriously high pheasant, what the great Raoul Millais calls a 'bathtub bird', because we luxuriate in the memory as we soak.

However wonderful the shoot, I can think of none where every drive is of equal standard, and where the pheasants always fly well. It is a fundamental problem of driven as against rough-shooting that because so many busy people are involved, once a date is set the shoot must go ahead, in anything short of dense fog or a snowstorm. Too often, guns are taking on pheasants in heavy rain, when the birds cannot offer a sporting challenge, and frankly the day should be cancelled. But it goes ahead because so much money and so many people's expectations are committed.

On a good, clear, windy high day, kindly hosts give guests a warm-up drive, where the odds against them are not too horrendous, before moving on to the toughest stands. A season or two ago, I found myself shooting at one drive in Yorkshire where I simply despaired. I was putting up the gun and firing cartridges, without the slightest hope that anything would fall down other than by fluke. Our host told us that the average for that drive through the season was a pheasant killed for every nine cartridges fired.

One day, shooting at Helmsley, I did something about which I shall be teased for a long time. I asked Dylan Williams of the Royal Berkshire Shooting School to come and stand behind me. We're trying to get better at this business, aren't we? Well, aren't we? And yes, I do know the old joke about the tycoon who stood on his peg one day with a shooting instructor, and was asked on his way to lunch whether he was bringing in his butler to show him how to eat.

On the peg, as you might expect, Dylan again and again faulted my gun mounting. 'You keep lifting your cheek off the stock. You're six, eight feet behind that bird. It's no

good rushing the gun up, then jerking it past the bird at
the last minute. You've got to have the action right all the
way through.' Dylan's coaching helped, I think. Would that
he was with me every day. I could bear the teasing. One
November shoot in Yorkshire the wind kept lifting and
then dropping all day, so that from drive to drive the speed
of the birds varied dramatically. All of us had trouble
adjusting our lead to cope.

The biggest problem when any of us is missing, any
shooting day, is that we don't know where. Dylan Williams
emphasizes the importance of making allowances for the
varying speed of the pheasants. Sometimes, when a bird
glided overhead, I was missing in front. It was the fast
curlers that were yards ahead of me. Dealing with very high
birds, one is at first bewildered by the measurable pause
between pressing the trigger and seeing the impact of the
shot. Those birds make one understand just how absurdly
slow, low and easy are many 'ordinary' South of England
pheasants.

Like most game shooters, I usually try to brush up my
technique at the beginning of the season, by making an
annual trip to the shooting school before I start practising
on the real thing. An hour at the clays is designed to boost
confidence. But most schools try too hard in this respect,
making the business too easy. Many times I have fired 75
or 100 cartridges and gone away puffing out my chest in
the belief that I have really cracked it. Then, on the first
day in a stubble field, the inaugural partridge streaks across
and I am reminded that any fool with an instructor beside
him can break a reasonable number of decelerating clays
approaching at forty feet or less.

Shooting-school teachers vary hugely in quality, and a
good many of those in business around the country are
simply not up to it. You give them your money, sometimes

set about changing the technique you have employed for years, and come home thoroughly confused – the worst possible frame of mind at the start of a season. Other instructors, of course, are stars. Like many people, I was a passionate admirer of Michael Rose, who taught at the West London for so many years, and whose brother Alan today carries on the tradition. Ken Davies at the Holland & Holland school, which offers the smartest set-up around London, has a big following. There are a few others like these around the country, whom everybody recognizes as the tops.

Often, I think, we do not give even the best teachers a fair chance, because a single session – and, with costs as they are, that is all many people manage – is simply not enough to hone a technique which will stand up to the pressure of high pheasants streaming past in a gale. I am one among many shooters who, on my day, can cope adequately with the average South of England pheasant. But I collapse under more testing conditions.

To try to diminish the number of fiascos, apart from taking Dylan Williams with me to a shoot on one occasion, I also put in several sessions with him at his school on the Thames escarpment at Basildon. I wanted to see what persistence could do for me. We started off on a sunny Saturday morning in August. As usual, I had little trouble with the first clays the trapper threw at me off the banks. We then tried a very entertaining ten minutes on the grouse layout, where a programmed sequence of thirty clays comes in singles, pairs and coveys – the most convincing grouse practice I have ever had.

But then we got to work on the high tower and, as usual, my problems began. 'For a start,' said Dylan, 'you mount the gun much too quickly. You can get away with that on easy birds but not with the tall ones.' I missed six or seven midi-clays in succession. Dylan asked the trapper to throw them full-sized. After a few, I begged him to go back to midis. The speed of the smaller targets seems infinitely more convincing – many of us have wasted hours practising on the bigger ones, which prove so little even if you hit them when they are slowing down. I would rather miss the midis than hit the jumbos.

'Let me show you what your mounting looks like,' said Dylan, taking up the gun. He wobbled an erratic circle towards an overhead clay. 'It's what we call a Magimix swing – you are chasing the bird all over the sky, then jerking the barrels past it at the last second.'

'Where do you think you missed that last one?'

'Behind, as usual, I guess.'

'About twelve feet behind.'

'*Twelve feet?*'

The most significant aspect of that session was that it made me understand just how far behind those tall birds I had been shooting.

'Don't mount the gun to the shoulder nearly so early,' said Dylan. 'Let the barrels follow your eye as the bird approaches, then put the gun up and swing through to fire when it's almost overhead.'

To adopt his technique meant changing deeply rooted habits. This is the essence of the relationship between any instructor and any pupil. There must be trust because each coach preaches a creed at least slightly different from that of his peers. Whoever you choose, you must follow his teaching implicitly to gain from the experience. Literally, you pay your money and take your choice. The average lesson of forty-five minutes or an hour seems quite long enough, given the risk of losing concentration. For most sporting shooters, clays do not excite that extra ounce of attention which a flying bird commands. Many men who get a reasonable amount of practice can make a respectable score against average English driven gamebirds. They are not that difficult in the absence of a strong wind. It is when we get into the higher reaches of the sport that poor coordination, from which I have always suffered, becomes a serious handicap.

We all know that rhythm and timing are what it is about. Shooting midi- and mini-clays seems by far the most effective way of creating realistic conditions to simulate high, fast pheasants or partridges. If a shooting school can teach me to do it, when I have spent thirty years accumulating every vice in the book, they can do it for anybody. The only certainty for almost every erring shooter, is that we shall never get there without a coach's help.

Whatever excuses one makes about missing high birds, one must acknowledge that those of us who get the chance to shoot game in those Devon or Yorkshire valleys are offered an immense amount of practice. Contrast the rough-shooter, who may only be given a chance to fire a dozen cartridges in a morning, with that of the man who lets off seventy or eighty cartridges in a drive. God knows, nobody presented with that many birds in succession can claim that he is denied a chance to correct mistakes. I shall always be grateful to the generous hosts who have invited me to the likes of Kepwick, Helmsley, Haddeo Valley and Dumbleton, for the opportunity to explore the upper limits of shooting in the most literal sense. I often argue that some shoots damage the cause of field sports by overdoing the bags. But I am hypocrite enough to admit that when one has the opportunity to shoot two guns at very high pheasants coming so fast that the barrels are burning through a glove, the excitement is matchless.

If I hit birds like that I feel I have accomplished something, especially those which one has to watch climbing,

climbing towards the line forever, as it seems, before they come within shot. If I miss them I brood for days, trying to work out what other guns are doing differently, what makes them succeed where I fail. Most of the answer is that they are not 6ft 5in tall and poorly coordinated. When I was in my twenties, I would sometimes watch a neighbour kill high pheasants beautifully, and think to myself, 'When I'm as old as he is, and I get as much practice as he does, then I shall shoot that well.' Nowadays, however, I look at the old gamebook and reflect on the fact that I get to fire perhaps four thousand cartridges a year. There is no excuse in lack of practice any more. There is no choice save to look at the mirror and think ruefully, 'This is as good as it gets.'

31

PLOTTING A COURSE

SOMEBODY WROTE RECENTLY that the great problem
for the designers of the Greenwich Dome is to come up
with anything to rouse in our children a sense of awe.
Our ancestors were indeed awed by the Great Exhibition.
Our parents and ourselves were at least respectfully
impressed by the Festival of Britain. What on earth can
one do now to provoke jaw-dropping among the young, for
whom the wonderful has become commonplace?

The other day I was lent a Global Positioning System
to try. It weighed half a pound and fitted comfortably into
my hand. I'm sure many of you are yawning and nodding

already, knowing all about these toys. But for the handful
of readers who are ignoramuses like me, I shall continue.
Switching on the GPS reveals a world map on a screen
maybe four inches by two. By pushing the button as often
as one chooses, it is possible to zoom in on say, Spain or
Italy or Britain, and keep zooming until the screen shows
the detail of a chosen bit of country. In my case, I found
Newbury and the M4-A34 crossover.

Fiddle for a second or two more, and the GPS provides
your precise position in degrees and minutes. A glance at
the Ordnance Survey map shows this to be correct within
a few yards – and I mean a few yards. Tinker a bit more
and the GPS will offer you a course to wherever you want
to go. Used in conjunction with map and compass (or even
without the compass), you need never be lost again, unless
the United States goes to war and switches off the guiding
satellite system. The Garmin GPS costs under £400, and I
am told other models are available in the US for nearer
£100.

Now, to me this gadget is literally awesome. I showed
it to my sixteen-year-old son. He thought it mildly
interesting. But he is fundamentally unsurprised by anything which technology proves capable of doing. Night-
vision sights, portable telephones, video cameras, computer-
generated graphics are regarded merely as the due of his
generation. That is the way things are now, and I suppose
always will be from here onward. We expect technological
miracles as part of the normal process of living. Given
that most of us are shooting with technology basically
unchanged since the late nineteenth century, I suppose it is
only a matter of time before some rich man turns up one
Saturday morning in Hampshire with, say, a laser-sighted
shotgun.

But one does not need to be very conservative to hope

not. Writing this, I turned with a twinge of nostalgia to an oddly shaped paperweight on my desk, a white pillar on a square green base. It was a gift to my father years ago, from the director of the Ordnance Survey. It is a model of that fast-disappearing artefact, the triangulation point. I think back to all those teenage corps cadet exercises, blundering about in thick mist and heavy rain on top of Welsh and Scottish mountains. It was a godsend, suddenly to see a trig point loom out of the murk. Every significant hill was crowned by one. A glance at the number on the base confirmed exactly which peak we had squelched and blundered our way to. A quick check on the compass sent us plodding on to the next.

Any politically correct environmentalist will say that, if we value nature as we should, the virginity of Britain's mountains will be restored if all those lumps of concrete planted on their summits are taken away, because happily mappers no longer need them. Perhaps they are right. But the passing of trig points represents another nail in the coffin of traditional navigation, with which I have had a lifelong love affair. I cherished the army prismatic compass, heavy old lump though it was – I think I've still got mine somewhere. As for maps, we all know that geography is somewhere down there with theology among the great cop-out subjects in any school, but from the first moment I saw a one-inch Ordnance Survey map, I was hooked. I never gave a stuff about groundnuts or Asian river deltas, but I adored mastering map symbols. The notion of a map as a perfect one-dimensional representation of a three-dimensional landscape gripped my imagination, as it does to this day. My cupboards are crammed with one-inch and two-and-a-half-inch maps of every tract of countryside in which I have spent significant time. I can browse happily over the contour lines even of hills I have never seen, conjuring up mental images of the spurs and re-entrants and river valleys and railway embankments which those compelling brown ripples portray.

Thanks to the Ordnance Survey, Britain is the best-mapped country in the world. American and European maps are miserable things by comparison, even the large-scale ones. When I lived in Ireland, the countryside never disappointed, but the awful maps of it did. If one is travelling by air or sea, there is nothing to beat the sense of security a first-class map provides. The mind boggles, to consider how our forefathers found their way in a world in which vast tracts were simply blank spaces on the chart – and that included much of Africa until barely a hundred years ago. It remains a fascinating experience, to twirl an eighteenth-century globe and ponder the great sweeps of *terra incognita* – I never forget the vivid examples one can glimpse in the Doge's Palace in Venice. I am a great fan of Patrick O'Brian's novels about Nelson's navy, in which people are always running aground on uncharted reefs, or searching for islands several degrees from where their discoverers had caused them to be placed on the chart.

As late as the Second World War, bomber pilots were often obliged to rely on the same wildly unreliable navigation technique as Nelson's captains – so called 'dead reckoning'. That is to say, if cloud or darkness made it impossible to shoot the sun with a sextant or to identify a landmark, one was obliged to estimate one's position simply by measuring the distance thought to have been covered since taking the last accurate fix, hours or days earlier. Given the difficulties of calculating wind speed and drift, dead-reckoning navigation caused many wartime pilots to drop their bombs not miles, but hundreds of miles from their objectives. Reliance on 'by guess and by God' explains why so many pre-twentieth-century sailors literally hit the rocks after a few days of gales and cloudy skies. I suppose it also helped to explain why young Hastings, looking for the top of Pen-y-fai with a large pack and half a dozen other sodden young men, so often ended up staring at the Clifton Suspension Bridge or Battersea Power Station.

But suddenly, all that is history. GPS systems, which featured in futuristic Bond movies thirty years ago, have become the present. As long as the battery doesn't go flat (which is a caveat that should be entered about almost every tool of modern life), we can discover exactly where we are by land, sea or air. A little romance has gone, but so too has a lot of time-wasting and risk.

My children simply want to know why we are so old-fashioned as not to have a GPS and electronic map fitted as standard in the car. Very soon we shall, my dears, we shall. Shed a tear for lost innocence – never again will it be possible to have those awful rows in the front seat, about which of the family is to blame for missing the turning to Cornwall. Any disasters – and of course, there will still be disasters – should all be down to NASA.

32

THE LUCK OF THE GAME

A GLASS CASE containing an unremarkable salmon caught my eye in a Shropshire gunroom. It bore an inscription: 'CAUGHT BY JANE ON THE SPEY 25 JULY 1995, AFTER 24 YEARS OF TRYING'. Suddenly, this banal fish achieved epic dimensions. Any of us, made aware of its pedigree, had to reflect with awe upon its significance for Jane, the sobs and euphoria and family sensation which must have convoyed it into the net.

But then go back a bit, and speculate (for I do not know the inside story) about the twenty-four seasons which preceded this piscatorial triumph: the countless hours of futile casting, the vain advice, the despair. It must all have seemed so wretchedly unfair, when everybody else caught fish. How could anyone's sporting luck be so rotten? And luck is what we are talking about, because everyone who has ever fished for salmon knows what a large part luck plays in who catches what, given a minimal level of competence and commitment.

I have been on both sides of the balance – catching more than my share for no reason anyone could discern, and catching nothing at all when some imbecile wife in the party (well, perhaps not imbecile, but you know what I mean) was hauling them out every ten minutes. Courtesy demands that, whenever a sportsman has more than his or her share of success, this should publicly be put down to luck: 'my peg just happened to be under the tap again' or 'we found ourselves bang in the middle of a shoal'. In private, most of us brood as we cast or wait on a stand about sporting luck, who gets it and why. 'Any luck?' we ask a fellow-fisher, when we are reunited over the luncheon basket. Now, this phrase is valid up to a point. If we find that a companion has caught, say, three fish to our two, then we can reasonably assume that he had a touch more luck. But suppose that he returns clutching five fish to our nothing, then we must begin to search our souls and wonder whether luck has anything to do with it. Be honest: he or she is probably a better fisher.

The first principle to grasp about fishing 'luck' is that 'to him that hath it jolly well gets given'. In other words, if you hear of some phenomenal haul on the Helmsdale, or a colossal bag on a grouse moor, it will sure as eggs not be Mick Spratt, the fishmonger who has saved up for twenty years for a glimpse of paradise, who finds himself on the receiving end, nor for that matter you or I. It will be a duke or a billionaire or a large-landed proprietor, because statistically they are the ones most likely to be out on the good days. I say this not out of social chippiness, but because years of research supported by a vast IBM database tell us that such is life. We simply have to hope God compensates for these injustices in other ways – say, by making sport's darlings of fortune not very good in bed.

Mind you, just to keep hope alive in other humble bosoms, I will now tell a contrary story. A while ago, I found myself sharing a river-bank with a well-known grandee whose luck was out that week. I caught a few fish. He didn't. He was not a happy bunny. Luck again, of course, but in his case for sixty-something years the luck had been going his way. He verily howled on this occasion, on finding that it was not.

In the middle of the week, I headed off to another river. The following Monday, my secretary reported with surprise that my erstwhile companion was on the phone for me. At once, I guessed what he wanted. 'How did you do on the Adder?' he enquired anxiously. 'Well, not great, I'm afraid,' said I. 'It was very hard pounding. We got seven in the end, but none over nineteen pounds.' A sob echoed down the wire. 'I caught *absolutely nothing*,' he said.

Now, truth to tell, I too had caught absolutely nothing on the Adder. I usually like to think of myself as a candid witness about my sporting achievements. But the temptation in this case was irresistible. If one is accustomed to seeing one's path flow as smooth as this legendarily pampered sporting guest, I imagine the carpet in the blue drawing room was dampened by tears for days over this impertinent rebuff from fate.

If we leave out the sort of luck that causes one to inherit a grouse moor or marry into a Devon pheasantry, for most of us shooting luck evens out through the season: a bad draw one day, a good one the next; rained off on Saturday,

brilliant sunshine a week later. All right, so you feel unlucky
if you have to glare into the sun through the best drive of
the day. At root, we all know that once you're out there
with a gun in your hand, the only thing that really matters
is how well you do your stuff and how sporting one is about
accepting the truth of this.

I take my hat off to an American friend, a very keen
shot, who sets us all an example about the luck of the draw.
'Have a good drive, Charlie?' I ask. 'Terrific! Marvellous!'
says Charlie. 'Only two grouse came over me, but they
were miles high, wonderful birds.' Approaching sixty, and
shooting thirty days a year at all sorts of grand shoots,
Charlie has preserved his enthusiasm, his capacity for
pleasure and absence of sporting greed in a way that makes
some of the rest of us blush. I am ashamed to look back
ten years or so and remember how mindlessly I shot at
anything that came my way on driven-pheasant days. I can
remember blazing away at pheasants low enough to graze
the grass as they passed me.

The success of a day's fox-hunting, by contrast, hinges
hugely on luck: the weather, the scent, whether they find,
whether your horse goes well, you lose a shoe or – rather
more serious – mislay hounds. With deerstalking it all
depends on where you are. Barring disastrous weather, there
are plenty of places in Scotland where any fool can shoot a
stag or three, from an Argocat if he chooses. Luck becomes
more important in those forests where deer are fewer and
the owner is selective about what gets taken out. Although
we always try to behave like little gentlemen in these
situations, it is pretty frustrating to spend hours getting
up to beasts, only to find there is nothing shootable among
them. I thought I was pretty unlucky a year or two ago to
hit a stag and kill a calf behind it. The stalker was a
seriously polite man, and stifled any public expression of

his views. But I was in no doubt that he considered this pure incompetence. Luck can be interpreted in all sorts of ways, can't it?

Among trout fishers, the ablest caster will almost invariably make the best basket. I submit that this is also true of low-water salmon fishing. I am a hopeless hand at the game because I lose faith in the chance of doing any good. Again and again, we see the canny caster winkle the odd fish out of the odd corner. Fishing for salmon on a decent river in good conditions, however, it is luck which overwhelmingly determines who catches most. Poor Jane, who suffered her twenty-four years of frustration, probably didn't need a new rod, more flies, casting lessons or even a different husband. She should simply have changed her rabbit's foot.

33

TOP DRAW SHOOTING

THE CHILLY DARKNESS receded to reveal a still, misty morning. The decision to shoot was just the right side of marginal. Relief gave way to anticipation, the sure knowledge that we were starting out for a great day, because every day up in those dales is great. Though I find a lot of Yorkshire birds hard to hit, for once I was not even nervous because I knew the place, our host and the other three guns well enough to lean back and revel in it all. Over the years, I have often written about the risks of overdoing shooting and of big bags. But now, for once, I shall write about the

big day, the sort of banquet most shooting men dream
about, at one of the half-dozen best driven-pheasant shoots
in Britain.

We were only five guns, because our host believes that
in an eight-gun line one or two are always out of it, which
can hurt on a four-drive day. There was a quarter-mile walk
across a field, and onward through damp woodland to the
first stand, because the birds in the bracken on the hillside
beyond were jumpy. The noise of vehicles could start a
stampede. Five, six, seven teams of beautiful black dogs
and their handlers dispersed to the rear, in themselves a
pleasure to watch setting about their business. The stops
eased forward. The shoot manager murmured into his radio
from the back of the line.

I was two, with my host on my right. Although it was
a cold day, I pulled off my coat to sit on my shooting stick
in a sweater; I find it hard to shoot fast wearing too many
layers. The dog was pegged. I plugged my ears with cotton
inside my ear defenders; I am embarrassingly deaf already.
My loader shouldered two bags, one carrying 75 cartridges,
the second 200. I pulled on my gloves and weighed a gun
in my hands. We were standing with our backs to a conifer
wood, looking up at a hillside of bracken fringed with a
game crop 200 yards in front. The beaters started moving
at a right angle towards us, the line 400 yards to our right.
The pheasants began to break forward, powering skywards
as they came.

I missed the first and second on my right; dropped the
next two overhead; then missed two really high ones; then
had a brief inspired patch at good birds curling left; more
overhead which I was hitting, more on the right that I was
still making a mess of. I glanced at the cartridge pile behind
us: perhaps 40 gone already, powder smoke hanging in the
still air, a few feathers drifting slowly out of the sky.

Furious action on the left and a lull in front. Two guns were shooting superbly, dropping the sort of birds I was missing, while one was struggling as much as I was. Few guns at this shoot, even the best, average much above a pheasant for four cartridges. Another big flush came straight at us. I was firing continuously, dropping birds that would be thought quite impressive in Hampshire, but still missing the best Yorkshire ones. I kept wasting cartridges on the right, dammit, while doing quite respectably on the left. Dropping my shoulder? There was no time to work it out.

The luxury of a day like this is that the flushes go on, and on, and on. Four out of five of the birds that came forward were worth shooting by any standard. Then, suddenly, the beaters and spaniels were converging in front of us and the whistle went. We sagged back, momentarily drained by excitement, and set about picking up. I had fired 93 cartridges.

For the second drive, we stood at the foot of an almost sheer, wooded hillside, once again with our backs to a conifer plantation. This is one of the best drives in Britain, and I never stop thanking my stars that I have a chance to shoot it – thirty years ago I would not have dared to hope. I was on the left flank, at five, a peg I had occupied before, where I knew birds would curl across me from right to left over the trees. On a day like this one has the chance to get a rhythm going, firing at the same pheasant again and again. However hard that bird may be, familiarity offers huge advantages to the gun.

The first pheasants swooped down from the mist-clad hilltop, flying fast, twisting and dramatically changing direction. A bang, then a couple, then a barrage, and within a few minutes we were all firing. I had the easiest draw, the place where most of the birds fly markedly lower than those on my right. But by South of England standards, every pheasant was a challenge. Glancing down the line, I could see some screamers coming down, but also a lot of birds lifting their tails, flinching, flying on. The picking up here is terrific, and the dogs got many of them 400 yards behind us. But this is the part of high-pheasant shooting which we all feel least comfortable about.

When birds are coming thick and fast, it is vital not to get into the wrong rhythm. Changing guns late, you find yourself leaning over backwards to fire at a bird, missing, then grabbing the other gun, and lo – you are firing late at the next one, and so on. Sometimes you fluke a bird down, but more often there is a succession of wasted cartridges. I kept reciting to myself the mantra: 'shoot in front, shoot in front' – and then forgetting.

The whistle. More than a hundred cartridge cases were lying behind me, and there was scope for a lovely bit of work for my dog in the wood on the left, which none of the pickers-up had touched yet. Paddy loses the plot amid the number of birds on the ground at a shoot like this, but I try to persuade him to ignore anything close at hand and concentrate on the long runners. Because everything is so impeccably organized, there is always time for picking-up – no hectic rush to the next drive.

Last before lunch. We were standing half-way up another steep hill, topped by a row of battered and blasted pines. Suddenly, maddeningly, the mist was closing in on us. The first birds were mere shadowy shapes up in the murk – but the drive was still just shootable. I was three, middle of the line, not shooting nearly as well as my neighbour, but surprising myself by some of the birds that were coming down. A lot of the hit ones were planing in behind us rather than throwing back their heads – another characteristic feature of high-bird shooting which makes me blush. This time, some simply would not face the mist, and glided by shoulder-high. Nobody even thinks of shooting at low birds here – who could want to, when there are so many magnificently testing ones?

It was over, with 77 cartridges scattered behind my peg. Everybody was chattering sixteen to the dozen about what a wonderful shoot they'd had. As we walked back to the vehicles for lunch, we felt euphoric, not least about cheating the weather. Our host was disappointed that the mist had deterred some of the birds from showing at their best, but none of the rest of us moaned about that. I was only grateful to have kept my end up, more or less, when often I feel completely outclassed by my neighbours.

For the last of the day, we were standing in a gully below another wooded hilltop, with another big wood behind. The morning murk had cleared. I was four, probably the best peg in the line, though with this drive you can never tell. Sometimes it works, sometimes it doesn't. Sometimes most of the birds favour the right flank, lower down. You never know till you start. I dropped my first bird high and left, and then another two or three. Thank God, I was having one of my good patches, and confidence does wonders for the next shot and the one after that. The pheasants came beautifully: not in big flushes but ones and twos and threes, steadily climbing over the guns, giving us time to take each at our own pace, yet seldom leaving more than fifteen or twenty seconds without a chance to put a gun up. Oh, the bliss, which comes so seldom to some of us, of performing decently at a steady stream of birds flying high, wide and handsome. Most were not quite as hard as those of the morning – over me anyway – but I basked in every moment of that glorious half-hour. At the end of it I had shot 40-odd pheasants, my loader told me I had fired 112 cartridges, and I had enjoyed one of the best days of my own shooting year.

Over two days on that trip to Yorkshire, I fired 635 cartridges. I have been lucky enough to go to that same peerless shoot maybe half a dozen times. Where does that leave my scruples about big bags? Still troubled, I must confess. But I have written about the experience because I try, in my scribblings about field sports, to embrace as wide a canvas as I can contrive from personal experience. The other day, I worked out that the average bag at the shoots I visited last season was 164. But that is as misleading as any average figure, because it reflects more than a few days with bags as small as 15 or 20, as well as occasions like those in Yorkshire, when they were a great deal higher.

At the big, high days I worry – as do most thoughtful shots I know – about the number of pricked birds which go on. That is the inescapable consequence of testing guns to their limits. On the other hand, shoots of this kind are run to extraordinarily high standards by the keepers and pickers-up. No trouble or cost is spared to pick wounded birds, to do the job properly from beginning to end. I love all those Yorkshiremen who beat and stop, flag and game cart, in a manner that is a model to shooting people. If all pheasant shooting was conducted on this scale, it would be bad for the sport and bad for the people who do it. I remain an impenitent advocate of the small days, the modest places, which represent the warp and woof of shooting, and upon which its future depends. But I cherish my luck, to have glimpsed its extravagant summits, to have known the thrill and challenge of what the best of the big shots lived for. This is not the sort of day which offers the thrill of the chase, but instead the thrill of a succession of wild half-hours of Rolls-Royce driven shooting.

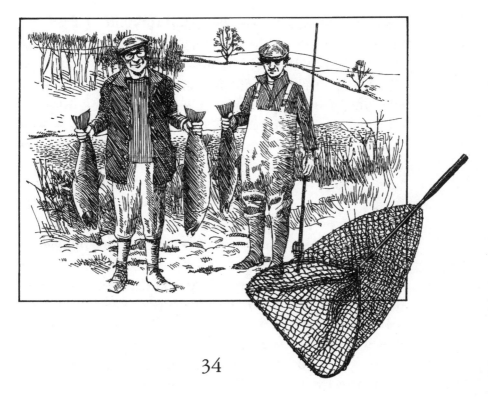

34

SALMON MAGIC

THROUGHOUT MUCH OF Africa the only measure of the seasons that matters is whether a day falls before or after the rains. So it was in Britain in the autumn of 1995 for a host of farmers, gardeners – and above all fishermen. Through those long, fruitless summer months we stared at almost waterless wadis. Fish gasped for life in pools almost barren of oxygen.

Then, at last, the skies opened and the rains came. In Scotland the parched heather moorland began to squelch beneath our feet in accustomed fashion. The rivers filled.

After the first floods carried away their three-month cargo of weed and debris from the beds, a glorious flow of peat-tinted water took its proper place between the banks.

Taking up a heavy salmon rod after months of frustration and disappointment seemed a solemn moment, together with wading into three feet of current where there were only rocks in July. I like to catch fish, but I also love merely to cast a fly, to bask in the rhythm of swinging a long line to and fro across a beautiful river, taking a pace downstream between every cast as I cover the pool. Salmon can be the most frustrating of all sporting quarry. If they are not in a taking mood – which few of them were through those hot summer months – they porpoise and leap all day a yard or two beyond the rod tip, indifferent to any temptation. But then, when the water rises and they start to move and respond to a lure, one watches every cast intently, waiting for that electric moment when the line tightens. Those who do not fish often ask fishermen what we think about as we wade. My own mind, at least, is focused solely upon the progress of this cast and the prospect of the next, measuring the eddies to guess where a fish might lie and aiming my fly accordingly.

Just before lunch on the first day, I was throwing a long line into the current, beneath the trees under the far bank, when a fish took. I lifted the rod, until it rested well bent in my hands, and settled to enjoy that peerless sensation of playing a salmon. As the fish made its first run, the ratchet on my father's old Hardy Perfect let out line with the scream of cogs that thrills every fisherman. I revelled in ten minutes of alternate retrieval and release, following the line downstream until at last the net slipped under an exhausted hen salmon. We admired it on the bank for a few moments and then lifted it gently back into the river.

It was evening before the next fish came, with a savage take and a run downstream that had me splashing and stumbling through the water in pursuit. This was one of the toughest fighting salmon I have ever met. For twenty minutes it leapt and wrenched at fly and cast, jerking the line beneath the water in a fashion that stops the heart of most fishers, fearful at every tug that the fish will win free. Finally, 150 yards below the point at which I had hooked it, I netted a lean, ugly 8lb cock that I killed for the pot.

Every salmon lie has a character of its own. All of us love to wade places that we have hunted for years, because every cast holds memories of fish lost or landed. Next morning I was casting across the fast water of one of the most beautiful and prolific pools on the river, a magnet to everyone who tries the beat. After only fifteen minutes on the water, a salmon took me and once more dragged me away downstream. The beauty of the setting accounts for much of the pleasure of Scottish fishing that it sometimes does not seem to matter if the pickings are sparse. But the thrill is all the greater if the scenery is matched by success for the fly. When I had lifted my 11lb fish on to the bank, I felt I did not mind if I failed to catch another all week. As it happened, I did catch a few more and so did our other rods, so everybody came home perfectly content. But just in case anyone who does not pursue salmon should suppose that it is always easy, let me tell you what happened on Friday.

A girl in our party had been casting vainly all week, with sagging morale and the added frustration of having lost a couple of fish. That afternoon she was working down a narrow stream. I had sent her to what I thought was the most likely taking pool on the beat, but she was finding it a tricky business to throw a fly on a short line under

overhanging trees on the far bank. I saw that she had caught
the fly in her hair and walked over to free it. Then I flicked
out her line under the trees and handed back the rod. The
line straightened as she lifted it to reveal a good fish well
anchored to the opposite end.

It was then that I should have gone home, handing over
guidance to the ghillie. Instead, in a flurry of jitters of my
own, I rattled out instructions: 'Wind him in now . . . Give
him line, give him line . . . Get your rod point up. Up! No
– down!' For at that moment the salmon leapt, revealing a
beautiful silver body, about 12lb. I leant over and slammed
down the rod point to prevent the fish breaking the cast,
then barked at the fisher to get the rod up again. My own
nerves had a disastrous effect upon hers. A few seconds later
the fish tore away downstream. On an impulse, horror of
horrors, *she put her hand across the whizzing reel winder.* She
checked its racing rotation dead in its tracks. In an instant,
the cast was broken. The fish vanished. The line hung limp.
To this day, my companion can't tell me why she stopped
the reel.

I wanted to cry. The frustrated fisherwoman did so. A
spectator from our team slipped off up the bank. He told
me later that he led away the ghillie with a firm assurance
that we were best left alone for a while, say two or three
hours. If there are few sensations to match the exhilaration
of hooking and landing a salmon, so there are few to surpass
the dejection which follows defeat. All of us will remember
that fish lost, long after we have forgotten the ones we
landed that week. I can recall in exact detail salmon which
escaped me in years past on Tweed and Shin, Naver and
Helmsdale. I never even glimpsed many of those fish, so
their size and shape remain a mystery to me, part of the
magic of hunting salmon.

It is always said that no one can call himself a fisherman

until he has lost his share of hooked fish. But that knowledge does nothing to diminish the pain, though of course it is the risk of separation from the prize which lends such irresistible excitement to success.

35

PORTRAIT IN MINIATURE

LET US FINISH with a small day: New Year's Eve on
Michael's 110 acres of grass, hedges and young plantations
on flat land looking west towards the Uffington White
Horse. We were six guns, Barry the forester on the neighbouring estate who nurtures 250 pheasants every year for
Michael, a pack of assorted dogs, and various wives and
children to beat. We dumped vehicles, dog leads and
gunsleeves. A belt of cartridges was more than enough, said
somebody. Michael gave us a little opening homily:

'*Don't* shoot the tame ducks off the pond, but you can
have a go at a wild one.' – Do we tell which are which by

asking them to introduce themselves? – '*Try* not to shoot Roger and Jasper, the cocks that run with the chickens. There'll be terrible tears if anything happens to them. Watch out for the barn owls. You can have a go at a woodcock – we spared them when there only seemed to be one or two on the place, but now there are quite a few.'

We set out across the grass fields, Michael justly proud of all his new broadleaf planting and the lovingly created hunt jumps – 'the way we do it here, there are always foxes'. We were deployed in the immemorial pattern for a day like this: three guns at the point of a hedge, three walking with the beaters up the willows and 20-yard-thick brambles and ivy-cumbered trees surrounding the remains of the old Wiltshire-Berkshire canal. I had been wool-gathering for ten minutes when a cock pheasant streaked past, four feet above the ground. I would have snatched a shot if I could, but he was past me and shielded by the hedge before I had even woken up. There was a double bang out on my left, the effect of which I couldn't see. A minute or two later Michael shouted 'over', and I took a cock overhead, which Paddy smartly retrieved. A minute or two more and there was another bird coming fast. I raised the gun confidently – and clean missed.

The pheasant was gone before I could fire the left barrel – and so was the damn dog. I whistled and shouted, to no avail. I knew what would happen next. The beaters reached us, and we all emerged just as Paddy came trotting back from 300 yards along the hedge, smugly bearing a hen pheasant and purring audibly as is his wont. 'Oh, you hit it after all,' said Michael. I replied sheepishly, 'No, I didn't. Paddy just believes that as long as he comes back with something, he's safe from a thrashing.' I called the killer to heel. We lined out across a young plantation. Only one bird came out of it, a hen flushed 30 yards out by Paddy, which I missed going away with both barrels. Giggles were discreetly muffled by the home team.

The next couple of drives were all but blank, to the dismay of Barry the keeper. We were within a couple of hundred yards of the farm boundary. He gazed towards the neighbour's wood and muttered darkly, 'Aniseed.' Over the fence, it seemed, they had their own ideas about how to encourage pheasants. Michael reckons to shoot four times a year, as well as Barry's day at the end of the season, and to expect an average bag of thirty – they pick up half what they rear. Everybody was cursing the deer and the damage they do to the new planting – roe are everywhere, and it is hard to keep them down. We set off along the next hedge, my turn as walking gun while the others headed it, a splendid pack of wild spaniels plunging through the cover, giving tongue in a fashion that would make a Cottesmore hound jealous. A hen rose steeply from a bramble patch. I dropped it behind, and watched an embarrassed Paddy beaten to the pick-up by one of the resident pack. I was whistling the dog when a partridge rocketed over the hedge to my left. I got the gun up late and missed it.

We trudged on across some waterlogged plough, a pound or two of chalky soil clinging to each boot. My companions were almost all family or neighbours, who knew the ground well and practically recognized each pheasant on sight. We gossiped about the state of the countryside political struggle. Michael told me a couple of bleak stories about a corporate shoot he had visited, where half the guns had never shot before. He told us about the hours he puts in every spring, pruning his trees with his own hands – all 5,000 of them. In a decade, he will have some wonderful avenues and hedges to show for it.

We dropped a bird or two here and there, missed a few more, and failed to get a shot at a covey of wild partridges that broke wide. Michael enthused about his experiences establishing the barn owls, starting with a rescued pair of road-accident casualties that were kept caged and fed only on day-old chicks, until they were old enough to return to the wild and start rearing local families. 'Did you know that cars are the biggest problem for barn owls? When they get up, their first two or three wing-beats are very slow, until they get into their stride.'

Another plantation yielded one more cock, bolted by Paddy from a hedge on the boundary. Almost all the surrounding shoots are in the same style as Michael's – modest affairs involving the farmer, a part-time keeper and a lot of walking. The country is too flat to show driven pheasants, even if anyone wanted to. He was being a generous host that day, putting me in the likely places. Heading the next hedge, I had plenty of warning as the spaniel pack approached, yelping triumphantly as a cock ran in front, took to the air, and fell on my left to an easy shot. A minute later the dogs scuffled another out, and I took it low over the next hedge, 20 yards out. Once again, to his chagrin, the spaniels beat Paddy to the dead bird – shame on him. But the ecstasy of being allowed to hunt the ground in front of me, to run for his life through those covers, was more than enough for him that morning. He was in seventh heaven.

Last drive. The beaters found a cock and a hen, which were dropped in succession on my right by Michael's sons. Total bag for the morning: 12. Total result: happiness. There were expressions of relief that Roger and Jasper had survived another day. We walked back to the house across the fields three hours after we had left it. Everybody including Barry came in for a jolly lunch. The home team said they were disappointed not to have seen more. I said that it had been one of the best days of the season for me, unclouded by guilts or doubts, savouring the flavour of the English countryside on a windy winter's day, letting off a dozen cartridges and taking one's chance at game in good company. What sportsman could ask for more?

CONCLUSION

BETWEEN THE DAWN of history and the nineteenth century, society's attitudes to field sports – hunting in all its guises – changed little. They were perceived as human activities natural as eating, sleeping, reproducing. 'The slothful man roasteth not that which he took in hunting,' Proverbs asserts with contempt, a biblical slingshot which we might use to advantage today against those too lazy to pick up properly or to cook what they kill for sport.

Delabere Blaine wrote in 1840: 'By field sports, we mean principally the chase after animals – the love of which, though thought cheaply by some, and blamable by others is, we are prepared to contend, inherent in our very nature.' Stonehenge admitted in 1875: 'It has often been said that field sports injure the moral and religious habits of the people . . . All pursuit of game purely for sport has an element of cruelty attending it.' But he satisfied himself that this stain could be subdued, 'and if possible, washed out, by the many counter-balancing advantages'. Stonehenge saw nothing 'which can injure the morals, or destroy that gentlemanly feeling which it should be the object of every true sportsman to encourage'.

Even in Victorian times, sportsmen recognized that the prime purposes of hunting in the early historical sense had been overtaken by the advance of society. As mankind has become not more civilized, but more urbanized, the need to hunt to eat has declined almost to vanishing point. The number of those with personal experience of hunting has diminished dramatically. We must also acknowledge that field sports have become a less natural, more artificial activity. Men no longer pursue wild creatures to extinction, but assist and nurture the survival of wild creatures in order to preserve quarry species.

'Common to all sports are certain basic principles,' wrote J. W. Dunne. 'These are not, as the uninitiated imagine, *devised* things; they are *discovered* things – discovered and rediscovered by generation after generation of sports-men actuated by no other motive than that of extracting the maximum pleasure and interest – from their pursuit, for example, was the discovery that it is always more pleasing and exciting to concentrate upon a selected, individual quarry – be this stag, or bird, or trout – firing into the brown is a poor form of amusement.' If it were not for sporting salmon fishermen, there would be no vigorous lobby to prevent the 'meat fishers', the high seas netsmen, from entirely destroying a great fish which their activities already imperil. Save for shooters, the red grouse would be rare in our wildernesses, and it has indeed become so on those ancient hills where sporting shooting is no longer an economic proposition. Wild birds of all kinds profit from the conservation policies of low-ground shooters. It is the proliferation of raptors, encouraged by environmentalists ill-disposed to shooting, which poses a formidable threat to the balance of wildlife in many areas of Britain.

The last half century, and especially the last decade, has produced an extraordinary increase in hostility to field sports, fired by a belief that the human pursuit of wild creatures for pleasure is inherently wrong. In the late 1980s, I was among those who deluded themselves that the new libertarianism inspired by Margaret Thatcher's premiership, the elevation of personal freedom, would halt this move-ment. We were wrong. Today, for reasons I have discussed in this book, the cause of 'animal rights' is being pursued with ever-increasing vigour. A kind of madness has overtaken some of those participating in the public argument. Otherwise sensible middle-class people in pet-obsessed Britain can be heard on the radio excusing acts of terrorism by animal rights militants, on the grounds that violence done to animals provides some excuse for retaliatory violence on behalf of animals, against people. In some circles it is thought perfectly understandable to transmute a fanatical enthusiasm for animal rights into hatred for one's fellow-men. The response to this sort of fanaticism, sad to say, is muted. A remarkable number of those who pursue field sports continue to ignore urgings to join country sports organizations and write cheques. Many of the abstainers are people who cheerfully spend thousands of pounds a year on hunting, shooting and fishing. Even now, they seem to believe that the threat can be ignored, that they can get on with doing their own thing without bothering to join the Countryside Alliance, the Game Conservancy, BASC. Their behaviour is both short-sighted and selfish. It seems incredible that when so many rich people hunt, shoot and fish, all the field sports organizations remain pathetically underfunded alongside the RSPCA, the RSPB, the League Against Cruel Sports, the World Wildlife Fund for Nature.

The opponents of field sports pay for huge advertising campaigns and sophisticated media advice, against which the modest sallies of our defenders seem like catapults against howitzers. It is not going too far to suggest that, if legislation is passed against hunting, shooting or fishing in the years ahead, we shall have only ourselves to blame, when many of us could not be bothered to lift heads from the stock of a gun, the neck of a hunter or the butt of a rod for long enough even to write a cheque to support the struggle.

I am not persuaded that the defenders of field sports choose their ground well. We make much of arguments about the number of jobs that would be lost if hunting was banned, for instance, and about the huge sums of cash generated for the economy by shooting and fishing. This case, a rational case, holds no water at all with the opponents of field sports, and not much with the public at large. The Scottish Nationalists are not going to spare grouse shooting merely because it is said to generate 2,300 jobs. The overall number of jobs, the absolute prospective economic loss, is not great enough to deter the foes of field sports. They care far more about alleged cruelty to animals than about mere money. This is a debate principally about the countryside and the environment, couched by the critics in intensely emotional terms. I believe we have a better chance of winning ground by highlighting the critical part field sports play in promoting the wider interests of wildlife and conservation. The meticulous research done by the Game Conservancy is invaluable. The most recent surveys at their test-bed estate at Loddington in Leicestershire, where they monitor wildlife densities on ground explicitly managed for game, as against those on land solely farmed for crops, shows a dramatic increase in populations of song thrushes and skylarks on the keepered estate. Harvest mice, in steep decline in so many places, are flourishing at Loddington, as are hares and wildflowers. Here, it is possible to make an argument that possesses a real resonance for the public, to fight on turf where we can make an impression on any but the most implacable opponent of field sports. The best hopes of us all for the future lie in persuading the uncommitted that field sports make a contribution to the environment that outweighs their supposed cruelty.

Reading some of my earlier chapters once more, I asked myself whether I had dwelt too much upon the past, and contrasted too brightly the historic pleasures of field sports with those of the present. But among the greatest pleasures of outside days for most of us is the sense of continuity with the experience of our sporting ancestors over the centuries. Our forefathers could take field sports for granted as part of the warp and woof of the countryside. They did not have to fight for them.

Yet for all my own devotion to the study of history, I am not nostalgic. We should not delude ourselves that the quality of life, even of country life, was better yesterday than it is today, save for a tiny minority of great landowners. No one familiar with the novels of Hardy, with Ronald Blythe's *Akenfield* or any realistic account of the lives of country people over past centuries can seriously propose that most people of departed generations were happier than we are now. Even such lyrical works as *Lark Rise To Candleford* paint a bleak picture of the harshness and austerity of village existence. I have mentioned above the shortcomings of rural communities sketched by George Eliot in *Silas Marner*. I have always been too nervous about being reincarnated as a ploughman rather than as a squire, to yearn to have been born one hundred or two hundred years ago, however many more grey partridges the stubbles could then boast.

No, instead let us celebrate the happiness still to be found on a hundred chalk streams, a thousand pheasant coverts, a host of rough shoots and heather hillsides. When I was young, my father doubted that I should see a fraction of the sport he had known. He was wrong. I cherish the same hopes for my children's generation, and for the future of Britain's countryside. If we take it for granted, we are lost. But if we never forget that we hold life leases on all manner of brilliant charms and pleasures, if we are willing to assert the claims of the hunters, even in this age of pavements and skyscrapers, then the pageant of field sports will survive and continue to flourish when we are long gone.

INDEX